SALLY COLLINS
Mastering
PRECISION PIECING

7 Spectacular Quilts with Techniques for Success

C&T PUBLISHING

Text © 2006 Sally Collins

Artwork © 2006 C&T Publishing, Inc.

Publisher: **Amy Marson**

Editorial Director: **Gailen Runge**

Acquisitions Editor: **Jan Grigsby**

Editor: **Liz Aneloski**

Technical Editors: **Joyce Engels Lytle and Wendy Mathson**

Copyeditor/Proofreader: **Wordfirm Inc.**

Cover Designer: **Kristen Yenche**

Design Director/Book Designer: **Rose Wright**

Illustrator: **John Heisch**

Production Assistant: **Tim Manibusan**

Photography: **Luke Mulks**, unless otherwise noted

Published by C&T Publishing, Inc., P.O. Box 1456, Lafayette, CA 94549

Front cover: **Lotus Flower**

Attention Copy Shops: Please note the following exception—publisher and author give permission to photocopy pages 59, 63, 68, 69, 72, 86, 87, 91, 92, 98, 99, 108–111, and 123 for personal use only.

Attention Teachers: C&T Publishing, Inc., encourages you to use this book as a text for teaching. Contact us at 800-284-1114 or www.ctpub.com for more information about the C&T Teachers Program.

We take great care to ensure that the information included in our books is accurate and presented in good faith, but no warranty is provided nor results guaranteed. Having no control over the choices of materials or procedures used, neither the author nor C&T Publishing, Inc., shall have any liability to any person or entity with respect to any loss or damage caused directly or indirectly by the information contained in this book. For your convenience, we post an up-to-date listing of corrections on our website (www.ctpub.com). If a correction is not already noted, please contact our customer service department at ctinfo@ctpub.com or at P.O. Box 1456, Lafayette, CA 94549.

Trademark (™) and registered trademark (®) names are used throughout this book. Rather than use the symbols with every occurrence of a trademark or registered trademark name, we are using the names only in the editorial fashion and to the benefit of the owner, with no intention of infringement.

Library of Congress Cataloging-in-Publication Data

Collins, Sally

Mastering precision piecing : 7 spectacular quilts with techniques for success / Sally Collins.

    p. cm.

Includes bibliographical references and index.

ISBN-13: 978-1-57120-363-2 (paper trade : alk. paper)

ISBN-10: 1-57120-363-X (paper trade : alk. paper)

1. Quilting--Patterns. 2. Patchwork--Patterns. 3. Machine quilting--Patterns. I. Title.

TT835C6473965 2006

746.46--dc22   2006011482

Printed in China

10 9 8 7 6 5 4 3 2 1

Dedication

For my friend Glorianne,
By your example, you gently teach me about acceptance,
patience, and following my heart. I am forever grateful for your
gifts of friendship, trust, and love.

Acknowledgments

As I wrote this book and created the projects featured in it, I was constantly reminded of so many friends, students, teachers, and family members who have personally and professionally encouraged, inspired, motivated, taught, listened, and guided me throughout the 28 years I have been making quilts. This book has truly been a collaborative effort by many individuals, and I am grateful to each of them. I regret that there is not room on this page to mention everyone.

Thank you to my husband, Joe, for his unconditional love and for always providing me with a safe, soft place to retreat; to all my students who encourage and motivate me to continue my quiltmaking journey; to my five "special" childhood girlfriends for their support and appreciation of my work; to Mary Brewer, Sharyn Craig, Joen Wolfrom, Jinny Beyer, Judy Martin, Marsha McCloskey, Judy Mathieson, Gai Perry, Diana McClun, and so many more who have inspired me both creatively and professionally to keep reaching higher; and, of course, to the staff at C&T Publishing for their guidance and expertise, especially my text editor, Liz Aneloski, and technical editor, Joyce Lytle, whose years of experience are reflected on these pages; and to Rose Wright of Graphic Productions for sharing her usual elegant style and taste in the design of this book. I am forever grateful to you all.

Contents

Introduction

I took my first quiltmaking class in 1978, and after being required to take a prerequisite class (I had never sewn before), I made my first real quilt. It was a queen-size sampler and I was so proud and excited I could barely contain myself.

Early in my quiltmaking journey I can remember taking as many classes as I could and making as many quilts as I could. I wanted to make them all. It didn't take long for me to realize that in my enthusiasm to create the projects, the *process* (how I was making them) fell through the cracks. I began to notice all the discrepancies, errors, and mistakes in my work. I began to feel disappointed in the results after investing so much time, effort, and expense.

So, I decided to commit myself to improving my workmanship through careful examination of *how* I was accomplishing the fundamental technical tasks of making a quilt. I detached myself from the outcome and focused on the process. I learned that mistakes are stepping-stones to improvement and success. I learned that good sewing has less to do with sewing perfectly than with knowing how to solve problems and how to get out of trouble. I learned to carefully examine my own work, identify common mistakes, determine why they occurred, and develop solutions to correct them—and now I'm sharing those solutions with everyone who reads this book.

The art of quiltmaking can be divided into three major components: design, color, and workmanship. Each has its own process. When I make quilts I start with design and color. I initially choose my design by sketching—using an existing design, graphing out my own, or combining the two. Then I choose my colors and fabrics. At this point I begin working with instant-camera photos, mirrors, and mock-ups to "see" the design and create a map or plan. I have an overall conceptual picture of the quilt in my head, but I specifically compose it in stages, always remaining open and flexible to change in order to create the best possible quilt.

Anything worth doing is worth doing well.

Once I see my quilt emerge through this process, I begin to cut and sew. I separate design and color from workmanship because this approach enables me to design and color freely without being encumbered by thinking about how I will sew it all together. Working this way also allows for serendipity to occur. My attitude is that I will get it sewn somehow.

As a traditional quiltmaker, my technical skills have always been the primary focus of my attention. As I have become more confident in and comfortable with those skills, I have come to understand that there is much more to quiltmaking than techniques and sewing.

This book is written for quiltmakers of all skill levels who are interested in advancing and improving their workmanship, design proficiency, and color skills to create beautiful quilts that excite the eye and challenge the hand. It is about improvement, not perfection. Seven projects are presented, in order of difficulty. To maximize your benefit, I encourage you to read through the entire section on process before beginning any of the projects.

I'm suggesting an approach to quiltmaking that rests on the value of spending the time necessary to achieve quality work. My hope is that you will appreciate the challenge of executing precise technique, experience the satisfaction of doing your best, and honor the work that gives your ideas a heartbeat.

Piece,
Sally

Achieving Quality Workmanship

"The greater danger for most of us is not that our aim is too high and we miss it, but that it is too low and we reach it."

Michelangelo (1475–1564)

It has been important to me to develop quality workmanship in my own quiltmaking. Why would I insist on having the very best machine, the best tools, and the highest-quality fabrics, and then not give my very best effort?

Whatever style of quilt you make, quality workmanship is just as important in the success of the quilt as color and design. Quality workmanship is the result of performing each element of the technical quiltmaking process with skill and care: cutting and sewing accurately; pinning appropriately; pressing effectively; matching seams and intersections exactly; evaluating, correcting, and measuring patchwork; and using appropriate finishing techniques. Focus on specifically *how* to accomplish a task rather than on *what* task is being accomplished.

The technical quiltmaking process is cumulative, interdependent, and each element is equally important and necessary to the whole. Success cannot be attained by sewing an accurate ¼″ seam allowance if the cutting is inaccurate. One element builds on the next. Each element has its own set of individual actions or steps necessary to accomplish it. Placing the focus on those individual steps creates a better understanding of each element and improves the level of skill at each step, resulting in self-confidence and competence. Knowledge replaces intimidation with confidence and competence.

Quality workmanship is a choice. You pursue it and develop it in your own work. I want to be clear: this does not resonate with every quilter, and it doesn't have to. However, if quality workmanship is your goal, you will find that it is the result of four factors:

HIGH INTENTION: You must want to achieve quality workmanship and be determined, committed, and motivated to maintain and sustain a high level of intention. Your goal must be to focus on the process rather than the project.

SINCERE EFFORT: Be willing to spend the time necessary to achieve quality work. It does not happen overnight. You must be willing to make mistakes, learn from them, and try again and again. The satisfaction of doing your best far outweighs the little bit of time it takes to make a correction. Growth and improvement come when we leave our comfort zones and push forward. Remember, you don't have to be right the first time, just the last time!

INTELLIGENT DIRECTION: Take classes, ask a lot of questions, and read those books we all buy (don't just look at the pictures). Choose not only project books, but reference books that tell you how to specifically execute various techniques—books that you will refer to over and over again, books that you can learn from so you can then use that information in your own way and in your own quilts.

SKILLFUL EXECUTION: Practice, evaluate your own work, learn to recognize mistakes, and learn how to correct them. It requires patience to keep working at something until it's right.

Achieving quality workmanship does not require any special talent; it is a learned skill that anyone who wants to and chooses to can acquire. I encourage you to choose well, choose quality, and continue to make the quilts you love.

Tools and Equipment

A craftsman's workmanship is a direct reflection of his choice of tools, the care he devotes to his tools, and his maintenance of these tools.

In addition to the usual quiltmaking tools, I also use the following to help me achieve quality workmanship.

- **Mirrors**: Two (5½″ × 11″ approx.) mirrors taped together on one side will enable you to see how borders will turn the corner, to reproduce one image multiple times, and to experiment with numerous other design uses. You can also go to your local plastic merchant and have any size mirror cut.

- **Instant or Digital Camera**: If you photograph work in progress, you can move and change the elements to get different looks and to evaluate value placement and other potential problems, and then move the work back to its original position without having to sketch or remember.

- **Multifaceted Viewer**: This is an inexpensive tool (found in toy shops) that allows you to view multiples of one block, on square or on point, and to see how the color is working.

- **Stiletto**: This pointed tool is used as an extension of your fingers when machine sewing.

- **Small Rotary Cutters**: Small cutters are easy to hold and control (use both 28mm and 18mm).

- **Olfa 12″ × 12″ Square Revolving Rotary Cutting Mat**: When subcutting or custom cutting small pieces or units, it is easier and more accurate to rotate the mat rather than moving and possibly disturbing the fabric. This is in addition to your usual mat.

- **1/16″ Hole Punch**: This is an invaluable tool for template making.

- **Pins**: I use two kinds of pins: Clover pins called Patchwork Pin (Fine) .4 mm, which are 20% thinner than .5mm pins, and IBC .5mm Super Fine Silk Pins #5004.

- **Rulers**: I use an Omnigrid 3″ × 18″, 4″ × 8″, and 4″ × 4″, all with a continuous ⅛″ grid marked with very fine black lines, both horizontally and vertically. These rulers are accurate and easy to read because even though I sew with ¼″ seam allowances, I often cut in ⅛″ increments. I also use 9½″ × 9½″ and 15″ × 15″ Omnigrid squares.

- **Reducing Glass**: This gives you distance from your work, which allows better evaluation of fabric, color, value, and design considerations.

- **Roxanne's Glue-Baste-It**: Get this water-soluble glue in the tiny bottle that has a permanent nozzle that doesn't clog.

- **Zippered Baggies**: I use various sizes for storing templates, completed blocks, blocks in progress, small design boards, or sometimes whole quilts, so they can be kept clean and can be seen and shared without being handled.

- **Straight-Stitch Throat Plate**: This throat plate is essential for straight stitching or machine quilting. It also prevents your machine from "eating" small pieces, because it is less likely that the fabric will enter the small hole than the longer slot in the usual zigzag throat plate.

- **Sewing Machine Needle**: I use a Schmetz Microtex 60/8 or 70/10.

- **Sewing Thread**: I use DMC Machine Embroidery Thread 50/2 in muddy gray or tan. This is 100% Egyptian long-staple, left-twist cotton.

- **Round Wooden Toothpick**: If a knot reappears on the top or back of your quilt, a toothpick is helpful in separating the cotton fibers and then pushing the knot back into the quilt.

- **Small Design Board**: Use an 11½″ × 13½″ foamcore board, covered with thin batting or flannel, for designing subunits or blocks. You can pin into it and take it to your machine. It fits into a two-gallon-size zippered baggie. This is in addition to an 80″ × 60″ design wall.

- **Serrated-Edge Scissors**: The 5½″ size is very helpful; these scissors enable you to maintain an exact straight line when trimming seams and cutting out fabric shapes for appliqué because the serration prevents the fabric from slipping off the edge.

- **Small Adhesive Sandpaper Dots or InvisiGRIP**: Placed on the backs of rulers, these help grab the mat and/or fabric and prevent slipping when cutting.

- **Clover White Marking Pen**: Use this pen for marking fine lines, dots, or quilting lines on dark fabrics; the markings are removed with the heat of the iron or water.

- **Spray Starch and Small Stencil Brush**: Brush starch onto the seam allowances of appliqué pieces before folding them over the template edges.

- **Freezer Paper, Toothpick, Small Iron**: These are necessary for appliqué templates.

- **Template Plastic**: Use ungridded, flat, and transparent plastic (so you can see through it) for making piecing templates.

- **Black Permanent Fine-Line Pen**: This is used for marking on template plastic and some fabrics. Do not use a Pigma pen because although it is permanent on fabric, it will smear on plastic.

- **Ott-Light**: I use the one that when opened is shaped like an L. I lay it on its side on my acrylic sewing table, positioned so that the light shines directly onto the side of the foot. It is critical when piecing to see exactly how your fabric is positioned under the foot (page 34).

Tools

Color and Fabric

*Pursue excellence ... There is great pleasure
and satisfaction in knowing you have
done your best work.*

Selecting a Color Palette

Selecting color and fabric is the most exciting, fun, and often challenging part of quiltmaking for me. It's what gets my heart pumping more than any other part of the quiltmaking process.

Our color choices give our quilts their personality and character, and they also reflect ourselves. When two or more people create a quilt from the same design or pattern, it is the color choices that distinguish one quilt from the other.

Whether we are making a quilt ourselves or viewing someone else's, we respond to color more than any other element in a quilt, so the objective is to create a quilt that is balanced in both color and design—a quilt that will embrace viewers from a distance and draw them closer. Color is what we see first, what demands our attention, and what we react and respond to emotionally (either positively, negatively, or indifferently).

Selecting color for quilts is a task that can make many quiltmakers, including myself, feel inadequate, inexperienced, and uncertain. We know that the technical steps of making quilts, such as cutting and sewing, are learned skills, but somehow we believe that choosing successful and harmonious color schemes and fabric combinations for our quilts comes from an artistic, ethereal place, unknown and unfamiliar to many of us. Through the years I have continued my efforts to improve in this area, and I encourage you to do the same if you want to choose colors more easily. Read books on color, take classes, and make lots of quilts. The ability to choose color well is a skill that improves and evolves with time, practice, patience, experimentation, and study. Not exactly what you wanted to hear, I know, but true nonetheless.

What produces the most satisfying results for me? Working with colors I love, seeing how colors relate to one another, always treating the process as a continuous string of decisions, and being persistent about not letting the choosing end until my heart sings. Improvement comes with experience. You have to be willing to try something new, make mistakes, and try again.

As you attend quilt shows or look at quilt magazines and books, deliberately and consciously notice only color and take physical or mental notes on what you like and do not like. Observe what color combinations you are drawn to. Are they toned, pure, pastel, bright, or quiet? Make note, as well, of what you do not like, as this is also valuable information. Determine whether your preference is for monochromatic quilts or two-color quilts—or maybe scrap quilts. Notice what appeals to you. Are you incorporating those traits or properties into your quilts? Are traditional-style quilts your favorite, or do art quilts appeal to you more? Through this analysis you will become more familiar with your own personal preferences and develop your own style. Noticing what you like and then determining how you can achieve that look is fun, exciting, humbling, and challenging.

Suggestions for Choosing a Color Scheme

- Develop a "color inspiration" file. Look through magazines, quilt-related or not—you might find inspiration in a catalog or home decor magazine. If you see a beautiful quilt, room, table setting, linen ad, or whatever in colors that please you, tear the picture out and place it in your file. It doesn't have to be a quilt to have a beautiful color palette.

This fabric was used only as a palette to choose color for *Lotus Flower*; it was never used in the quilt.

● Use a fabric with beautiful colors, regardless of print or content, as inspiration—even if you never use the actual fabric in your quilt.

● Choose colors for a quilt based on its purpose, or the reason for making it, if there is one—for example, a holiday or seasonal quilt (Christmas: red and green; Easter: pastels; autumn: earth tones). If it's a gift for a friend, you might use his or her favorite colors.

● The quilt style can determine the color choices. Maybe you want an Amish-style quilt (rich, dense solid colors), or an old-fashioned country style (browns, tans, pinks), or a Victorian style (blacks and pinks), or a contemporary style (bright, bold colors).

● Nature always offers a beautiful variety of palettes such as seascapes, seasons, flowers, foliage, and so on.

Inspiration for color is all around us. Begin to see with color in mind. Once you have an inspirational image or object (magazine page, fabric, feeling, holiday), use it to choose your colors and fabrics. Look at your inspirational image and identify each color you see in it. Examine it carefully and do not miss any subtle colors.

Begin to pull fabrics in those colors from your personal resource center (or the quilt shop shelves). Keep proportion in mind as well. If your inspiration object is mostly pinks with a few greens and just a touch of gold, build your palette accordingly. Make your fabrics look like the inspiration piece you are using and maintain its color integrity, character, and proportion.

Now take each color and expand it to increase its potential. For each color, develop a range of values from light to dark with the intensity that is apparent in your inspiration. Vary the visual texture or size and style of the print on the fabric to develop a good variety, and include a bright and a very dark. You do not have to use every fabric; you are just developing a full palette with lots of choices. This is one of many ways you might develop color for your quilt. It's the one I use most often.

Colors and fabrics chosen from center palette fabric for *French Confection* (page 60).

Sometimes I simply want to try a new combination of colors, as I did for *Fleur-de-Lis* (page 76). Purple is not a color I use often. It was challenging for me, but I still developed my palette the same way, by choosing a variety of visual textures and values. Sometimes I want to work in a particular combination of colors, as I did for *Pieceful* (page 100). For that quilt I wanted to work in all neutrals. Right after making that decision I saw a picture of a painting that communicated exactly the feeling I wanted to create, so I cut it out and took it with me as I developed my palette. I still included a variety of values and visual textures.

Noteworthy

Early in my quiltmaking journey, when I would find a multi-colored fabric to use as a palette, I'd buy two or three yards because I was taught that it was supposed to be used for the border as well. However, as I have gained experience, I have found that when it comes time to choose fabric for the border, the palette fabric is rarely the best choice. I used to use it anyway because I had it. Now when I see a beautiful multi-colored fabric I may want to use as a palette in the future, I buy only an eighth or quarter yard and use the fabric for its color information to build my quilt, but I never actually use the fabric in my quilt. This offers the opportunity to collect lots of palette fabrics for inspiration!

Using the Color Wheel

I encourage you to become familiar with and develop a basic understanding of the color wheel. This understanding has helped me realize that even though I rarely use the exact colors on the color wheel, they are the source from which my choices emerge. You will begin to understand that colors opposite one another on the color wheel are complements; they make each other look their best, so when you are looking to make a two-color quilt or for something to accent your quilt, look across the color wheel to find the right choice.

Two, three, or four colors that are next to one another on the color wheel (analogous) work beautifully together, and the accent is across the color wheel. This was my strategy for *Fleur-de-Lis* (page 76). I initially chose purple and its neighbors (magenta, pink, and blue); then for the background I went across the color wheel and chose light peach.

My quilt *French Confection* (page 60) is loosely based on a triadic color scheme of blue, yellow, and pink (every fourth color on the color wheel) and is also a very successful color combination.

Pieceful (page 100) is an achromatic (no color) color scheme. Monochromatic (one color) is always a very good choice for a color scheme as well.

These are just a few of the many possible ways to choose successful color combinations for your quilts using the color wheel. A word of caution: too many colors can sometimes create chaos, while selecting only one or two colors but using many values and visual textures gives a calm, organized, smooth appearance. When in doubt, simple is always best! Start somewhere—read books on color, take color classes—and begin your journey toward developing your own color style.

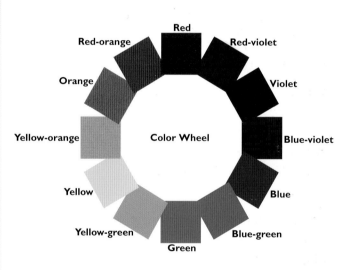

Value Placement Creates Design

Value refers to the amount of lightness or darkness in a color (hue). Adding black to pure colors creates shades (dark values). Adding white to pure colors creates tints (light values). Adding gray to pure colors creates tones. Shades, tints, and tones of color are all values ranging from light to dark. Value is also relative and relies on the surrounding values to define itself. For example, what we think is a medium-value fabric becomes light when surrounded by dark and becomes dark when surrounded by light. Value placement is what creates design, although color gets most of the applause.

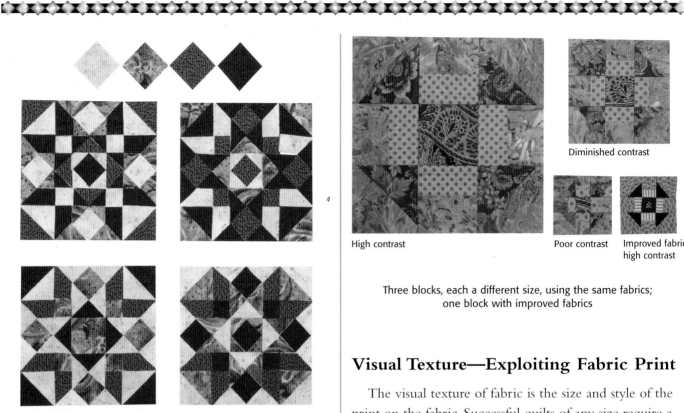

Value placement creates design.

Diminished contrast

High contrast   Poor contrast   Improved fabrics—
                                                  high contrast

Three blocks, each a different size, using the same fabrics;
one block with improved fabrics

Visual Texture—Exploiting Fabric Print

The visual texture of fabric is the size and style of the print on the fabric. Successful quilts of any size require a variety of visual textures to create interest. Quilters have an enormous number of options and choices in visual texture today. Be sure your fabric resource center includes most, if not all, of them. Large, medium, and small floral; foliage-type fabrics; plaids, stripes, and checks printed regularly or irregularly; and dots, circles, geometrics, and paisleys—we need them all!

I find it helpful to cut out shapes (in the sizes I use most often) from a 3″ × 5″ card and use the windows in the card to help show me how fabrics will look cut up. I place the card on bolts of fabric when I shop or when pulling fabric from my own shelves. (Using this card technique will also help clarify how light or dark a color will appear once it's cut to the size you need.) Using a variety of visual textures in quilts or blocks is what adds interest and detail. Just remember to create balance, not chaos. If I have a busy printed fabric in the background, then my design-area fabrics are quiet, and vice versa. You don't have to love every fabric you buy; choose some fabrics just because they are interesting in color or have interesting lines.

Tone-on-tone fabrics usually feature two or more values of one color, with subtle but effective visual texture. They can read as solids from a distance, have low activity, and add interest without distraction. I use this type of fabric most often.

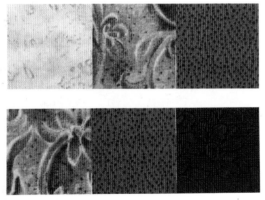

Value is relative.

Value Contrast Defines Design

Value contrast is the difference in lightness and darkness between a shape and what is positioned next to it. You can develop high, exaggerated contrast or low, subtle contrast. Intricate, small piecing especially benefits from high, exaggerated value contrast, which allows the viewer to clearly read the design from a distance. It's important to note here that the smaller you cut the colored piece, the darker it appears. The intensity or saturation of color is how pure and brilliant or how grayed and dull it is.

3″ × 5″ card with shapes cut out to see how fabric will look cut up

choosing a busy multicolored fabric that can break up the shape, be distracting, and confuse the eye. Using multicolored prints in intricate piecing can create chaos and results in the inability to decipher the design and/or individual shapes.

Visual texture used creatively adds interest, unexpected detail, and integrity to all quilts. I am always trying to maximize the visual texture of tone-on-tone fabrics. I avoid fabrics that have random areas of white in them since they can be distracting and can fall in areas of the piecing (for example, at the tip of a triangle against a light background) that can make good sewing look poorly done.

I also collect border prints and consider using them on most of my quilts. They add elegance, sophistication, and detail. See *Pieceful* (page 100) and *French Confection* (page 60).

I rarely use multicolored prints in my quilts because they compete with the intricacy of the piecing. If you are working with small pieces, use quiet, tone-on-tone fabrics that will fill the shape with color and texture rather than

Sampling of my preferred fabric styles

Helpful Strategies

As I compose blocks or quilts, I think about or evaluate several things when my work just isn't looking the way I think it should. Try incorporating one or more of the following ideas and see if it might help your work too. I do know from experience that often the smallest change can make the biggest difference.

- If you find that your eye travels all over your quilt, try adding a very dark fabric of one color. This helps to anchor the quilt while giving it order, unity, and a restful place for the eye.

- If your block or quilt seems dull or flat and uninteresting, add a bright (high intensity) value of one of the colors, in small amounts. A little goes a long way.

- Evaluate and determine whether your block or quilt seems too busy and chaotic. You might need to quiet your block or quilt by replacing some of the busy print fabrics with lower-activity quiet fabrics. Remember that if you have a great fabric to star in your quilt, you will need to surround it with quiet, supporting-role fabrics in order to be able to appreciate the star.

- View your work through a reducing glass; if anything really pops out, that is usually the area that needs to be changed. Maybe the color is right but the value or intensity needs improvement. Maybe the contrast is too exaggerated or too subtle. I also find it critical to view my quilts from at least twenty feet away. What looks really good close up (even using a reducing glass) can look dull, flat, and uninteresting from a distance.

- Perhaps the proportion of your colors needs improvement. Equal amounts of all your colors can create confusion. I usually have one dominant color, then a secondary color, and then an accent color used in small amounts. Good color proportion will help create balance and order. Usually, blocks have mostly background color, then design-area color, and then an accent color is added in smaller areas. Proportion in size and scale of prints is also a consideration.

- Don't expect to make all the right choices initially; just get something on your design wall and then you will have something to change and refine.

- One, two, or three colors in a variety of values and intensities can often be more successful than lots of different colors. Some of the most beautiful, spectacular quilts are monochromatic. Keeping it simple is always a good choice.

- If you have difficulty deciphering the design, try exaggerating the contrast.

- If your quilt looks ordinary, try using a color for the background rather than a typical "quilterly" light fabric.

Becoming comfortable with and understanding color is an ongoing, continuous process, and your skills will improve with practice. When I choose color and fabric for quilts and blocks I still sometimes feel like I'm flying by the seat of my pants, but I've learned to step out of the box, freely make mistakes, learn, and improve. Frustration is now tempered by fun, excitement, and challenge. I encourage you to refer to the books on color listed in the bibliography (page 125); they have all helped and inspired me on my color journey. If I can do it so can you.

Fabric Preparation

I recommend using only high-quality 100% cotton fabric. Cotton is dependable, manageable, soft, easy to finger-crease, and substantial in weight when sewing; it also presses well and is a must for intricate piecework. Having said that, understand that cotton fabric is fluid and moves as you cut, sew, press, and quilt. Be aware of that and forgiving of yourself as you make your quilts, blocks, and garments.

My personal preference is to prewash and dry my fabrics. I do not do anything special: I wash and rinse my fabric on a gentle cycle, then I put it in the dryer on medium to low heat. From the dryer, I fold the fabric and place it on my shelf. I press only when I'm ready to cut and use it.

I usually purchase third-yard pieces of fabric. If I need fabric for borders, I buy enough fabric to use the length grain because it eliminates stretching and ensures successful straight borders. If I find a fabric I can't live without, I buy three yards.

Fabric Grain

The grain of fabric is the lengthwise (warp) and crosswise (weft) threads that are woven together to create the fabric. Cross grain runs from selvage to selvage, shrinks more than length grain, and has some stretch, depending upon the thread count of the fabric and the weave. Length grain runs parallel to the selvages and has very little shrinkage and no stretch. Both crosswise and lengthwise grains are also described as straight of grain. Keeping the straight of grain on the outside edges of your blocks or quilt is critical to maintaining accurate measurements and keeping the work square.

Random bias is anything other than crosswise or lengthwise grain and has some stretch. True bias runs at a 45° angle to the crosswise and lengthwise grain and has the maximum amount of stretch.

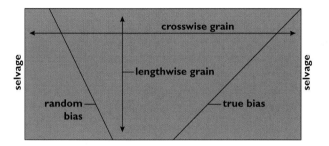

Noteworthy

To please the eye, directional fabrics should be cut with the print or pattern of the fabric rather than the grain if a discrepancy exists between the two.

When using templates, grain arrows should be aligned with the straight of grain (crosswise or lengthwise). Bias edges can stretch, create ripples and waves, and be difficult to control. However, I never sacrifice fabric design for grain. If I want a particular motif or part of a fabric to be positioned in a certain way that results in exposed bias edges, I handle it and sew it very carefully. I am extremely respectful of bias and keep the iron away from exposed bias edges whenever possible.

Successful quiltmaking—regardless of project size—requires careful attention to grain placement. The blocks, projects, and techniques described in this book will be specific about grain.

Design

*Take the time necessary to give your
ideas a heartbeat.*

Design Principles

What is design? Design means executing a plan. It is the arrangement of details that make up a work of art. We often look at quilts and immediately know, intuitively, whether they are successful or not. However, we might not always be able to identify why they are successful or unsuccessful. Whatever your quiltmaking style, specific design principles must be followed in creating successful quilt design.

- *Value* is the amount of light or dark in a color. Value placement is what actually creates design and is the most important principle. How and where we place the dark, medium, and light colors in our quilts creates the design and enables the viewer to decipher and read the design. How large or small the value difference is between two values that touch is called contrast. As you examine your quilt when designing, consider the value. Does it seem to all mush together? Perhaps you need more exaggerated value contrast in some areas to clarify the design. Does it seem choppy and sharp rather than smooth? Perhaps creating more subtle or lower contrast in some areas will solve the problem. It is always helpful to look at your quilt from a distance. Use a reducing glass, look at a photo, or get at least twenty feet from it.

- *Color* is what gets all the attention and applause. It gives quilts their personality and defines our personal style. Color determines whether the quilt is bold, dynamic, soft, rich, whimsical, and so on. There are no hard-and-fast rules about choosing color combinations, only suggestions, so if you are pleased with your choices,

continue. If you feel something might be missing or your choices could be improved, refer to the Color and Fabric chapter (page 11) for some ideas. At the end of the day, it's your quilt and if you are pleased with the results that is all that matters.

- *Texture* is created through the quilting stitches, the fabric type (silk, cotton, flannel, etc.), the size and style of the print on the fabric (stripes, plaids, florals, dots, etc.), embellishments (buttons, embroidery, beads, etc.), or any combination of these elements. Quilting texture is apparent in *Fleur-de-Lis* (page 76).

- *Shape* or *form* is anything that has width and height, such as circles, triangles, squares, rectangles, leaves, flowers, and so on. I think the most beautiful quilt designs combine both straight and curved lines, although one should be dominant over the other to prevent chaos. *Petite Sirah* (page 88) embraces both curved and geometric shapes in the design and the quilting.

- *Line*: Lines in quilts can be either curved, straight, jagged, or a combination of these.

- *Scale* is the size of one shape relative to another. Different sizes of shapes in quilts create interest.

- *Direction* means that the design moves or draws the eye vertically, horizontally, or diagonally. Many of my quilts are symmetrical, medallion-style quilts and have a radial direction, as in *Lotus Flower* (page 112).

Think of these design principles as ingredients in a recipe. Each has its own purpose, taste, and property. In a recipe, if one ingredient is used too much or demands too much attention, or if you leave one out, the whole recipe can fail. This is true in design as well. If the design adheres to all the principles and is balanced, the quilt will be visually successful—or, in a word, delicious!

Good quilt design is achieved when you mix and blend the design principles to create harmony, unity, balance, and variety. Unity holds a quilt design together. We need some visual organization or a relationship between the elements. In *Petite Sirah* (page 88), unity is created by repeating the same red and purple background, which allows for the variety of color in the Dresden Plates and the pieced border.

When unity is lacking, quilts can seem disconnected, confusing, and chaotic. Unity is accomplished through repetition of the design elements. Repetition of a particular design element gives a sense of order, but you must also be careful not to create monotony. Variety is necessary and enhances design as well as creates interest for the viewer. My quilt *French Confection* (page 60) is a repeat-block quilt and employs only three colors (turquoise, red, and yellow), but using many values of those colors and many visual textures of fabric creates variety and prevents monotony. Both unity and variety are necessary for successful design. When one is not present the design will suffer.

These are just some simple, basic guidelines for creating design. In the end, reading, taking color and design classes, practicing, and experience are always the best teachers. However, remember that there are always exceptions to every rule, so learn to follow and trust your heart and make quilts you love.

Drafting

I am always grateful that my entrance into the quilt community took place at a time when drafting, making templates, and scissor-cutting fabric were the most commonly applied techniques. Drafting has enabled me to better understand the workings of a design—to clearly see how the design fits and sews together—and allows me to be more creative and original.

The following introduction to drafting will help you advance your design skills. Refer to the bibliography for further study.

The following tools are needed to begin drafting:

- Accurate graph paper divided by 8-to-the-inch and 10-to-the-inch lines, with darkened one-inch lines

- A No. 2 mechanical pencil (the disposable ones work fine)

- A good eraser (do not rely on the end of the pencil)

- An accurate ruler: 2″ × 12″ or 2″ × 18″ C-Thru ruler with red lines and 8-to-the-inch grid divisions (purchase at an art supply or drafting store)

- A good compass (the cheaper ones do not always hold their position)

- A 6″ or 12″ draftsman's triangle or square ruler, depending on the size of work you do

Drafting tools

Most patchwork designs fit into or are developed on a grid. The grid refers to the squares (in this case) that a block pattern is divided into, much like a checkerboard. Shapes (triangles, rectangles, parallelograms, etc.) are then developed or superimposed over the grid by connecting or eliminating lines to create the design.

There are four basic grid-drafting categories that much of patchwork fits into: four-patch, nine-patch, five-patch, and seven-patch. The drafting category means that the block is divided into exactly that number of total divisions or multiples of that number.

Successful pattern drafting begins with the ability to look at a block design or pattern and visually divide it into equal units or sections or grids. The easiest way to determine what drafting category a block pattern falls into is to count the number of equal divisions across the top or down the side of the block or along one long seam, or go to the smallest piece and count.

If you count two, four, or eight equal divisions, your block would be in the four-patch drafting category and the number of equal divisions would give you the appropriate grid formation to then develop your block pattern.

2x2 grid

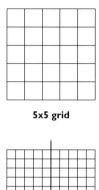

Broken Dishes

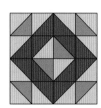

4x4 grid

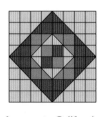

Hour Glass Variation

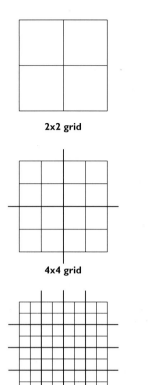

8x8 grid

Journey to California Variation

Four-patch

If you count three, six, or nine equal divisions, your block would be in the nine-patch drafting category and the number of equal divisions would give you the appropriate grid formation to then develop your block pattern.

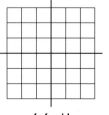

3x3 grid

Ohio Star

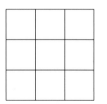

6x6 grid

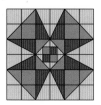

Road to Paradise Variation

Nine-patch

If you count five or ten equal divisions, your block would be a five-patch and the number of equal divisions would give you the appropriate grid formation to then develop your block pattern.

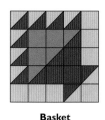

5x5 grid

Basket

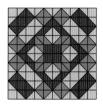

10x10 grid

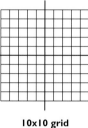

Unknown

Five-patch

If you count seven or fourteen equal divisions, your block would be a seven-patch and the number of equal divisions would give you the appropriate grid formation to then develop the block pattern.

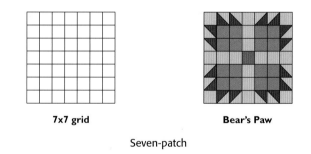

7x7 grid

Bear's Paw

Seven-patch

Another very common drafting category is the simple eight-pointed star, wherein the design or block is developed from lines radiating out from the center of a square rather than an equal grid of squares. This is discussed on page 25.

There are other drafting categories that are not discussed here, such as five-pointed star designs, hexagons, more advanced eight-pointed star designs, and so on. The information presented here is intended to serve as a stepping-stone for you to begin the drafting process and own your own work.

Noteworthy

Quilters are often confused about what *finished* and *unfinished* mean when block sizes are stated in books and patterns. To clarify: *finished* indicates the block size without any seam allowances included (e.g., a 3˝ finished block); *unfinished* indicates the block size including a ¼˝ seam allowance on all sides (e.g., a 3½˝ unfinished block). Whenever you are drafting, designing, calculating, or figuring out anything, seam allowances are never included. Seam allowances are added only when it is time to cut and sew.

To begin drafting, follow these steps:

1. Choose a block design you want to make (for this exercise we will choose a Sawtooth Star). Your preferred cutting method (rotary cutting or templates) and personal sewing skill level will influence the type of pattern you choose. The more complicated the block (this often has to do with how many pieces are in the block), the more sewing skill is required.

2. Determine the drafting category or basic grid of your chosen block design (is it a nine-patch, four-patch, five-patch, seven-patch, or eight-pointed star?). The Sawtooth Star's drafting category is a four-patch with a 4×4 grid.

3. Decide on the size of block you want to make (we will draft a 6˝ block). Although blocks can be drafted in any size you desire, it is easiest to choose a size of block that is easily divisible by the number of grids across or down the pattern. For example, if you are designing a four-patch drafting-category block with a 16-square grid (4×4), it could be easily drafted into a 4˝, 6˝, 8˝, 10˝, or 12˝ block size because those sizes are all divisible by 4. Similarly, if you have chosen a nine-patch drafting-category block with a 36-square grid (6×6), it could be easily drafted into a 3˝, 4½˝, 6˝, or 7½˝ block size. All are easily divisible by 6.

4. Draw the chosen size of square on graph paper. For this exercise draw a 6˝ × 6˝ square on 8-to-the-inch graph paper. You would use 10-to-the-inch graph paper for five-patch drafting-category blocks and when your numbers work out in tenths.

Noteworthy

When using a pencil and ruler to make lines exactly on graph paper lines or to connect corners and dots exactly to make perfect diagonal lines, you must position your ruler's edge slightly away from the specific area to allow for the width of the pencil. Also, to see clearly and avoid creating shadows when drafting, direct your light source onto the side of the ruler where your pencil is.

5. Determine the basic grid dimension and draw the grid within the 6˝ × 6˝ square. The grid dimension is the measurement or size of each division of the square. For example, for our exercise, we are drafting a 6˝ Sawtooth Star that is a four-patch drafting-category block (4×4 grid). To determine the grid dimension, **divide** the size of the block (6˝) by the number of equal divisions (4). That is, 6˝ divided by 4 divisions equals a 1.5˝, or 1½˝, grid dimension. (I work on a small handheld calculator to figure out my numbers.)

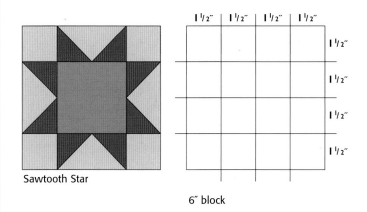

Sawtooth Star

6˝ block

Noteworthy

You could easily change the size of your block by changing (or choosing) the grid dimension. For example, if your grid dimension is 2˝, you would **multiply** 2˝ (grid dimension) by the number of equal divisions (4), which yields an 8˝ block. If the grid were 1¼˝, you would have a 5˝ block; if the grid dimension were 3˝, you would have a 12˝ block. **Multiplying** the grid dimension by the number of divisions determines the size of the block.

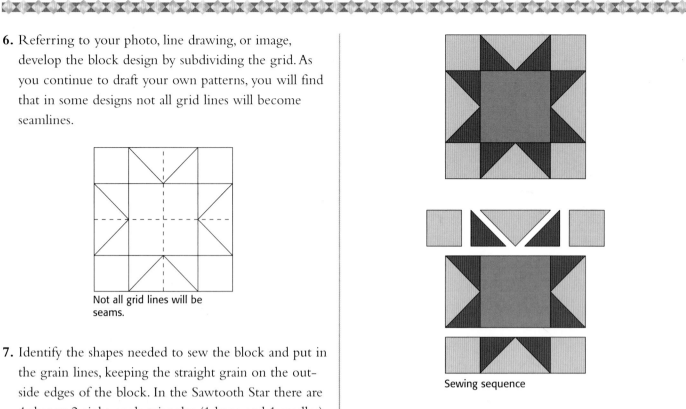

6. Referring to your photo, line drawing, or image, develop the block design by subdividing the grid. As you continue to draft your own patterns, you will find that in some designs not all grid lines will become seamlines.

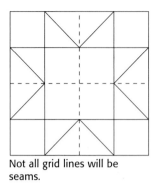

Not all grid lines will be seams.

7. Identify the shapes needed to sew the block and put in the grain lines, keeping the straight grain on the outside edges of the block. In the Sawtooth Star there are 4 shapes: 2 right-angle triangles (1 large and 1 smaller) and 2 squares (1 large and 1 smaller); these are shapes A, B, C, and D.

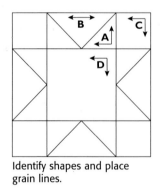

Identify shapes and place grain lines.

8. Examine the design and determine the logical sewing sequence to piece the block. One way to do this is to first find the longest lines (usually, but not always, they will run from edge to edge horizontally, vertically, or diagonally). Blocks are usually assembled by first joining pieces into units, then units into rows, then rows into the completed blocks.

Sewing sequence

9. To be able to sew the design, you now need to determine the cutting dimensions by isolating the shapes, adding a ¼″ seam allowance on all sides, and then measuring the shapes. When measuring a shape for cutting, if the dimensions are easily found on the ruler then rotary cutting would be the preferred method of cutting. If the size is not easily found on the ruler (for me this is anything beyond ⅛″ increments), make a template for that shape (page 31). For example, the A triangle is a 1½″ finished half-square triangle (1½″ on the short sides). If you want to be able to cut a square in half that will yield 2 triangle shapes that include a ¼″ seam allowance on all 3 sides, simply add the ¼″ seam allowance on all 3 sides of the triangle, measure from corner to tip, cut your square that size, and then cut the square in half diagonally.

Sometimes you read about so-called magic numbers, like adding ⅞″ to the finished size of your half-square triangle to get the size of square you need to cut in half diagonally. There is no magic. If you simply add the ¼″ seam allowance on all sides of a right-angle triangle and measure it from corner to tip, you will see that the ⅞″ measurement exists. The extended tip created when you draw around the right-angle triangle always measures an additional ⅜″ beyond the ¼″ we expect to be there.

This is always true. In this case you would cut a square $2\frac{3}{8}'' \times 2\frac{3}{8}''$ and cut it in half diagonally to create 2 shape A triangles.

The same is true for cutting quarter-square triangles, except that here the magic number is $1\frac{1}{4}''$. If you isolate and measure the long leg of the quarter-square triangle shape B in our 6″ Sawtooth Star block, for example, it measures 3″. Add a $\frac{1}{4}''$ seam allowance on all 3 sides and you will be able to cut a square the finished size (3″ × 3″) plus $1\frac{1}{4}''$ (or in this case $4\frac{1}{4}'' \times 4\frac{1}{4}''$) and cut this square into quarters diagonally. Again, no magic. The measurement exists if you measure from tip to tip; you are adding an additional $\frac{6}{8}''$ ($\frac{3}{8}''$ on each extended tip) to the usual $\frac{1}{2}''$ seam allowance.

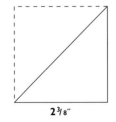

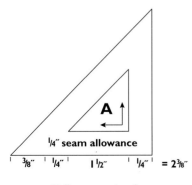

Half-square triangle

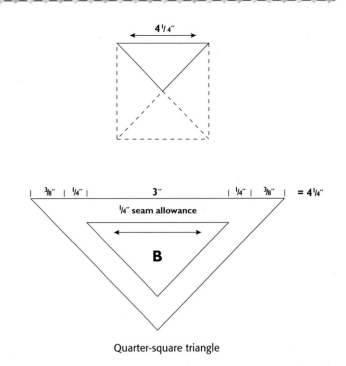

Quarter-square triangle

That is where those so-called magic numbers come from. It's no mystery—the measurements are there. You will always add $\frac{7}{8}''$ to the finished short side of a half-square triangle in order to get the size of the square to cut 2 triangles that include a $\frac{1}{4}''$ seam allowance on all 3 sides. Similarly, you will always add $1\frac{1}{4}''$ to the finished long side of a quarter-square triangle in order to know the size of the square to cut 4 triangles that include a $\frac{1}{4}''$ seam allowance on all 3 sides.

For shape C, you will cut a 2″ × 2″ square ($1\frac{1}{2}''$ grid dimension plus $\frac{1}{2}''$ for seam allowance).

For shape D, you will cut a $3\frac{1}{2}'' \times 3\frac{1}{2}''$ square (shape D takes up the space of 2 grids, so it measures 3″ × 3″ plus $\frac{1}{2}''$ for seam allowance).

10. Choose your color and fabric and begin to accurately cut and sew.

How to Draft Any Size Square into Any Size Grid

Sometimes you will want to draft a block that does not easily fit into the size of the square you want to work with. For example, if you want to draft a 6″ Bear's Paw block, which is a seven-patch drafting-category block (7×7 grid), you need to divide a 6″ × 6″ square into 7 equal divisions across and down, or 49 total. On a calculator, 6 divided by 7 equals 0.857, which is not a ruler-friendly number and which, unless you have

7-to-the-inch graph paper, is challenging to draft accurately. The following describes a way to accurately divide any size square into any size grid.

1. Draw the size of square you desire (in this case a 6″ × 6″ square) on any paper, graph or not, and label the 4 corners 1, 2, 3, and 4.

2. Find a measurement on your ruler that is larger than the block size and that is also divisible by 7 (the number of equal divisions across and down). That would be the 7″ mark on your ruler. Seven is divisible by 7 and is larger than the 6″ block you chose (7″ divided by 7 equals 1″).

3. Position one end of your ruler on the left #1 corner of your 6″ × 6″ square. Angle the ruler up until the 7″ mark is on the right side line of the square.

4. Make a dot on your paper every 1″ (this is the number you arrived at by dividing 7 into 7 in above). Mark exactly, not casually.

5. Position the drafting triangle or square ruler on the bottom edge of your paper as well as on the first dot, backing off the edge of the drafting triangle or square ruler to accommodate the pencil. This creates an accurate 90° angle. Draw a vertical line going right through the dot. Repeat for all the dots across the square.

6. Turn your paper a quarter turn and repeat Steps 3–5 to complete the 7×7 grid in the 6″ × 6″ square. This grid will allow you to draft the Bear's Paw block or any 6″ seven-patch block.

Noteworthy

If the number you need doesn't fit on the square, just extend the right edge line upward to accommodate the ruler to reach the desired number.

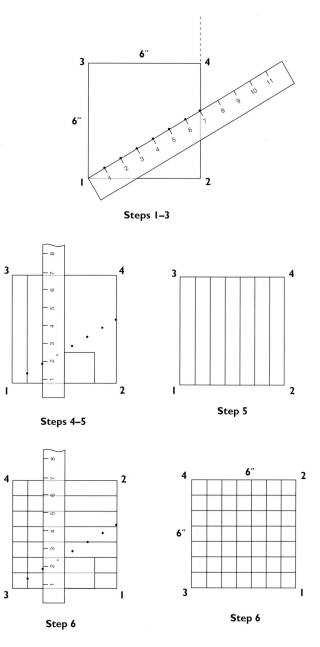

Steps 1–3

Steps 4–5

Step 5

Step 6

Step 6

6″ × 6″ square divided into a 7×7 grid

How to Draft a Simple Eight–Pointed Star

1. Draw a square of any desired size on graph paper or plain paper.

2. Draw light lines diagonally, horizontally, and vertically on the square. This identifies the center and gives needed reference lines for drafting.

3. Place the point of your compass at the center and open the compass so that the pencil is at one of the corners. Hold this position on the compass.

4. Now move the point of the compass to the left corner and swivel the pencil so it lightly marks the 2 lines that extend from that corner.

5. Repeat for the remaining 3 corners.

6. Label these markings A and B, as illustrated. Connect each A to 2 Bs and erase the appropriate lines to clarify the 3 template shapes needed for a simple eight-pointed LeMoyne Star block: a square, a triangle, and a true diamond.

7. Notice that the equality present in this category is not the distance between the 3 divisions along the edge of the block but the distance from one star point to another.

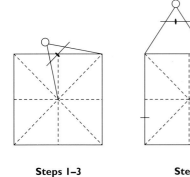

| Steps 1–3 | Step 4 |

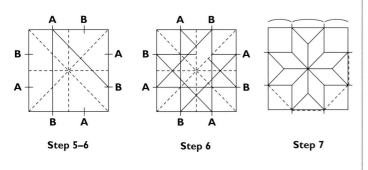

| Step 5–6 | Step 6 | Step 7 |

Eight-pointed star

How to Measure and Monitor Patchwork

Most square patchwork blocks are developed on a grid of equal divisions across and down a square. Grid dimension refers to the size of each individual square and determines the size of the block.

To be able to measure your work as you sew, you must know what the grid dimension is. You could determine this information in two ways.

1. Decide the block pattern you want to design (Sawtooth Star), identify the drafting category (four-patch, 4×4 grid), and choose a block size (6″). Then, to determine the grid dimension, simply **divide** the size of the block by the number of equal divisions across the edge of the design. For example, 6″ (block size) divided by 4 (number of equal division across the block) equals a 1½″ grid dimension.

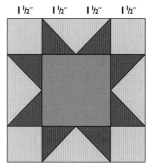

6″ Sawtooth Star block

2. Another way to determine the grid dimension of a block is to choose it. For example, let's say you want to make a Sawtooth Star block (four-patch, 4×4 grid) and you are comfortable sewing in a 1″ finished grid. The block size is determined by **multiplying** the grid dimension (1″) by the number of equal divisions across the block (4), so 1″ × 4″ equals a 4″ block size. I sometimes choose the grid dimension if I'm making only 1 block or if I'm doing a repeat-block quilt, because then the size of the block is not as important as working in a grid dimension I'm comfortable with. I also sometimes reduce the grid dimension when I want to challenge myself and practice more intricate sewing.

If the grid dimension plus seam allowance is not ruler-friendly (the smallest fraction I use with rulers is eighths) and I'm using templates for cutting, I use the template to evaluate and monitor the patchwork. Refer to Accurate Templates (page 31) for clarification.

Let's assume we are now going to sew the 6″ Sawtooth Star block that has a grid dimension of 1½″ (remember, the grid dimension does not include seam allowances). The fabric is cut and includes seam allowances, the units are created, the block is laid out, and you are ready to sew row 1 together. To begin you would sew the first 2 units of row 1 together.

To measure your work, follow these steps:

1. Add up the number of grids you have sewn together.

2. Multiply the number of grids sewn by the grid dimension.

3. Add ½″ for seam allowance, always.

Noteworthy

When measuring, whenever a shape or unit takes up the space of more than 1 grid, it gets credit for the number of grids it occupies.

This means that for the Sawtooth Star block, 3 grids × 1½″ equals 4½″, plus ½″ for seam allowances equals 5″. The first 3 grids of row 1 should measure 5″ from edge to edge. If they do, great; if they do not, either the cutting or the sewing is in question. Do not continue adding grids until the first 3 measure 5″. When these 3 grids measure 5″, forget this number and continue.

Add the next unit of row 1 to those already sewn. Now you have added another grid, so to measure your work, repeat Steps 1–3. Row 1, from edge to edge, should now measure 6½″ (4 grids × 1½″ grid dimension equals 6″, plus ½″ for seam allowances equals 6½″).

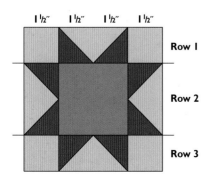

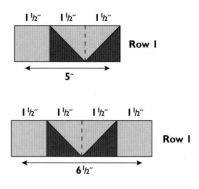

If it does, great; if it does not, correct it. If you remain faithful to this system, and measure after adding each piece or unit, you will be able to identify where your discrepancies are because they must be in the last seam you've sewn.

To maintain the grid dimension established for the block, you can take only a ¼″ seam allowance off each side of the accurately cut pieces, and you must take ¼″ off—no more and no less. Additionally, the smaller the pieces you are sewing, the less tolerance for error exists.

Is measuring your work as you sew worth the time it takes? Yes. This is how I sew all the time, in any scale, large or small. It is not fun to get three rows of a block sewn and discover when you go to join the rows that the intersections don't match and the rows are different lengths, which means the outside edges of the block will be uneven. All are unacceptable scenarios when striving to achieve quality workmanship.

In the project instructions, I provide grid dimensions wherever relevant. When using templates to monitor your work, refer to Accurate Templates (page 31).

Rough-Cut Mock-Ups

I use mock-ups as a design tool to compose my work, piece by piece, and interview color and fabric placement in blocks or quilts before the actual cutting and sewing take place. In the past, I was too impatient to bother with mock-ups and wanted to get right to the cutting and sewing. As I have gained experience, I have learned that taking the time to create mock-ups is invaluable to my process. It is not fun to get a block all cut and sewn and then, upon closer evaluation, discover areas where the color and fabric choices could have or should have been corrected or improved upon. Taking the time to compose and interview different colors and fabrics is fun and exciting, and it allows for serendipity to emerge.

An important element of making mock-ups is recognizing that you do not have to be "right" the first time. You just need to put something down and then begin the process of change and refinement. You must put something—anything—down first, and then begin to improve, compose, change, and follow your heart. It is an opportunity to explore the "what if" possibilities. What if I change red to blue, change the light to dark, change the floral fabric to a stripe? Creating mock-ups is a creative, challenging, and exciting opportunity to explore ideas and compose your quilts without being encumbered by the sewing process.

Because I usually do intricate work with small pieces, I cut fabric for my mock-ups in the pieces' actual size, without seam allowances, because I can more accurately evaluate how the colors and printed fabrics will look cut up and next to other colors and fabrics. As stated in the Color and Fabric chapter, color becomes darker the smaller it is cut, and a 3″ × 5″ card with small shapes cut out will help you know how prints and colors will look that size.

My experience has been that often a very small change can make a great deal of difference. After the design, color, and fabric choices have been made using mock-ups, the focus turns to the technical process. Always keep an open mind and remain flexible and willing to change.

I'm interested in accumulating as much color, value, fabric, and design information as possible before I cut and sew, but I can also be impatient at times. If the block design is symmetrical, you only need to mock up and compose one-half or one-quarter or one-eighth of the block and then use mirrors to see the whole design.

The term *rough-cut mock-ups* refers to cutting shapes by eye rather than exactly. For example, if I'm making the 5″ tree block in *Fire Fly* (page 67), I use the grid dimension (if applicable) to know the finished size of the triangles to cut (if the grid dimension is ½″, I cut lots of ½″ × ½″ squares and cut them in half diagonally and compose one-half of the tree). If you are using templates, place the template on the fabric, make dots through the punched holes, and then scissor-cut from dot to dot. If the finished shape is close to a ruler-friendly number, round it off and rotary cut. Remember that this is a rough-cut mock-up. Make it easy on yourself. This

should be an instructive, fun, and simple exercise to help you gather and evaluate information and make informed choices. I do not cut up the background fabric but instead move my rough-cut pieces to different background fabrics or cut more pieces to see different background options. I work on a flannel-covered foam-core board, referring to the block diagram to position the triangles. When you have placed the triangles on the board, position the mirror so it faces the half-tree mock-up, allowing you to see the whole tree. Move and change the triangles until the tree you see in the mirror meets your standards.

Mock-up of half the tree

Using a mirror to see the whole tree

One diamond mocked up

The Lone Star block in the *Lotus Flower* project (page 112) is another candidate for mock-up and mirrors. You will cut 16 small diamonds and place them appropriately on a potential background fabric, referring to the diagram, and then surround 2 edges with the mirrors to see the whole Lone Star.

Begin to notice when your work is symmetrical and take advantage of mock-ups and mirrors in your design process. This is an exciting, challenging, useful, and creative technique. Explore. Have fun. It's not always where we are going or how fast we get there that matters so much as the road we take.

Using mirrors to see the whole star

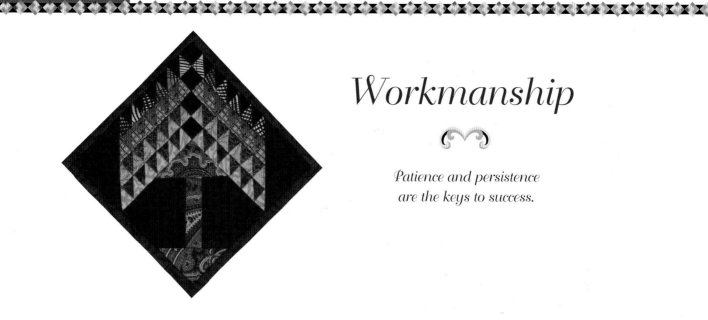

Workmanship

*Patience and persistence
are the keys to success.*

Evaluate and Correct Patchwork as You Sew

We can have the most beautiful designs coupled with delicious color palettes, but if we want to make quilts, we eventually have to sew—and I believe how well we sew matters.

The technical process includes cutting accurately (whether using a rotary cutter or templates), sewing with an accurate ¼″ seam allowance, pinning and pressing, keeping edges aligned, sewing straight, measuring and monitoring your work as you sew, and using appropriate finishing techniques. This process is an accumulative one, not a singular one; each part must be done well and in concert with the others in order for the finished project to be successful.

Certain technical sewing errors occur repeatedly, and these are the ones I will discuss in this chapter. One word of advice before we continue: carefully evaluate your work as you cut and sew, and remain vigilant during each step of the process. If you find discrepancies when your quilt top is complete, that is not the time to evaluate, nor are "squaring up" or "quilting it out" valid correction techniques. Pieces or units that are inaccurately cut and poorly sewn will result in inaccurate and poorly sewn blocks and quilts.

The goal is to achieve quality workmanship within the scope of our own personal standards. We are each responsible for our work, and improvement, not perfection, is what we are seeking. Good sewing is not about sewing perfectly each time we sit at the machine. Good sewing is knowing how to get out of trouble when we get into it.

That means we need to evaluate, critique, and correct our work as we sew. Being able to identify problems, understand and know what went wrong, and then know how to correct the problem is still important for me. Mistakes are simply a brief departure from success. They are part of the process, and once you recognize and accept that, you begin to see them in a different way. We will always make mistakes. The important thing is what we do about them. Mistakes are more about learning and moving forward than looking backward in time.

The following criteria for evaluating your work will help as you strive for improvement.

- Blocks/quilts are well pressed, clean, and tidy on both the front and back.

- Blocks/quilts are square. Outside edges are even and straight.

- Blocks/quilts include a ¼″ seam allowance on all outside edges.

- Value placement reflects an easy-to-read, clear design.

- Visual texture of fabrics is interesting and varied without being busy and chaotic.

- All points are complete and sharp.

- All seam intersections are matched.

- Equality of same shapes is maintained.

- Straight seams are straight, not wobbled.

- Curved seams are smooth, without pleats or points.

- Triangle points are the same height, if relevant.

- Seam allowances are trimmed, if relevant.

- Straight grain of fabric is on outside edges of blocks/quilts.

- Borders are straight and flat, not wavy or ruffled.

- Corners of blocks/quilts are 90° and square.

- Quilting is even and balanced over the surface of the quilt.

- If binding corners are mitered, the folds are stitched closed on both front and back.

- If binding corners and border corners are both mitered, the miter seams match.

How to Sharpen Essential Sewing Skills

Accurate Drafting

Accurate drafting of designs and pattern shapes is critical. Check and double-check your drafting, numbers, measurements, and angles before cutting, and always make a sample block before cutting out the whole quilt. If you are using pattern shapes from books or other sources, always measure (finished size) the two edges of each shape that will be joined to be sure they are the same size and will sew together smoothly. Never assume they are correct. A simple check with a ruler on the paper can save time and frustration when you sew. Another way is to cut up paper rather than fabric to do this preliminary checking. Accuracy and quality begin here, and you must be working with accurate shapes and patterns. Patchwork is like a puzzle; all the pieces must join together smoothly and exactly.

Accurate Cutting

Noteworthy

Accurate cutting, whether you are using templates or rotary cutting, is essential. If your fabric pieces are cut just $1/16''$ off, over only eight pieces you will have accumulated a discrepancy of $1/2''$—and you haven't even begun to sew yet.

Accurate Rotary Cutting

In my own personal experience and many years of teaching, I have found six specific areas that can be considered for improvement when rotary cutting.

1. One area of concern is how to place the ruler onto the fabric for cutting. Many quilters position the ruler so that the 1″ line on the ruler is just touching or butted up against the raw edge of the fabric, and then they make their cut. When you do this, you lose the width of the 1″ line on the ruler every time you cut. To cut correctly with a full, maximum measurement, you must lift the ruler up and place the 1″ line (or whatever the dimension you are cutting) onto the edge of the fabric, because an accurate 1″ measurement includes the 1″ line on the ruler. The line should lie exactly on the edge of the fabric; don't overcompensate and have fabric showing to the left of the line. If you are using Omnigrid rulers, I am referring to the black lines, not the yellow lines.

   Including the dimension line on the ruler when rotary cutting accomplishes two important things. First, thread takes up space, so including the line on the ruler when you cut gives the thread a place to be; and second, including the line on your ruler when you rotary cut eliminates the need to sew with a scant $1/4''$ seam allowance, whatever that is! Cut with a full measurement and sew with a full $1/4''$ seam allowance, measuring $1/4''$ from the tip of the needle out to the right, which becomes your seam guide (foot edge, tape, etc.).

2. Another common problem with rotary cutting that contributes to inaccuracies and injuries is starting to roll the cutter before you're really set up to cut. Position yourself comfortably in front of the mat and fabric, position the ruler and your hand on the ruler comfortably, then place the cutter blade a little before the fabric area you will be cutting and next to the ruler edge, pressing down so that the blade is on the mat, and then begin to roll the cutter.

3. How you position the cutter can also be a concern. Position the rotary cutter at a slight angle inward, so the blade is positioned exactly where the fabric and the ruler touch, which ensures a more accurate cut. This also prevents veering off to the right, away from the ruler edge and into the yardage. I usually cut only two layers of fabric at a time to maintain accuracy, and I use two different sizes of mats: an 18″ × 24″ for larger cutting and a smaller, 12″ × 12″ square Olfa mat that revolves 360° for subcutting, which enables me to keep my fabric in place as I rotate the mat.

Position the cutter at a slight angle.

4. Unless you are physically impaired, always stand when you rotary cut. If you sit and rotary cut you have no leverage; your vision is undermined because you are looking across the ruler and fabric, rather than over and down; shadows are created; and as you extend your arm to cut, the cutter comes away from the edge of the ruler, resulting in inaccuracies.

5. Change the blade often. As soon as you start going back and recutting areas or threads, or pressing or working too hard, it's time to change the blade.

6. Rulers that move while you are cutting result in inaccuracies. To prevent this, put either sandpaper dots or InvisiGRIP on the back.

Accurate Templates

I know that many quilters are opposed to designs that require templates because they never seem to work. The problem is the drawn line. Any time you draw a line next to or along a ruler's edge or template edge, you make the shape larger. The templates I make, which are described here, never use that line. You will cut the seam allowance onto the template, and then you will rotary cut the fabric using the template so that the template and the fabric and the pattern are all exactly the same size. I promise that these templates, if made as I describe, will be the most accurate templates you have ever used.

Templates are wonderful, powerful tools that give great rewards and improve our potential for both quality and custom work. I use templates if the shape I need is a size not easily found on my ruler, if it is oddly shaped or curved, if I want to custom cut a particular design area

from a fabric once or multiple times, or if I want to custom cut from a strip unit. Accurate templates that include a ¼″ seam allowance ensure accurate work. Templates support total freedom in design; they help you align two pieces for sewing by pinning at reference dots marked on the fabric pieces; and they help you monitor sewing accuracy because they reflect the sewing line. As I sew, I place the template on the sewn units; the seamlines and the lines on the template should match.

When templates are needed, I mark the sewing line on the templates and punch a hole wherever a line changes direction, which allows me to insert a marking tool through the hole and make a dot on the fabric. These dots are used as reference guides when pinning one shape to another, so the pieces are aligned properly for sewing, and to aid in Y-seam construction. When making templates, I use a permanent black pen to mark dots, sewing lines, identifying information, grain lines, and any other necessary information. If you make a marking mistake, a Q-tip dipped in a little nail polish remover or Goo Gone will remove it.

To make a template, have an Olfa Touch Knife or X-ACTO knife; ungridded, flat, transparent (see-through) template plastic; a rotary ruler; a mat; a small (18mm or 28mm) rotary cutter; ¹⁄₁₆″ hole punch; and masking or painter's tape on hand and follow the directions below.

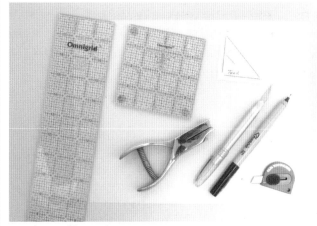

Template-making tools

1. Place a manageable-sized piece of template plastic over the pattern shape needed. You can tape the plastic in place to eliminate any slipping or shifting. Be sure you have allowed adequate room to add the seam allowance. Mark a dot wherever a line changes direction; then, with a ruler edge, ALMOST connect the dots, leaving them obvious and apparent for piercing or punching. To do this, position your ruler edge so the dots just sit on the ruler edge and mark the lines to almost connect the dots. These lines, if continued, would pass right through the centers of the dots. You will place the template over your sewn work and match these lines to the seamlines on your pieced unit to monitor accuracy.

2. Write the identifying letter or number, block or design name, size, and grain-line arrow on each template. These markings are very important, not only for the obvious informative reasons, but because they identify the right side of the template.

3. To add a ¼″ seam allowance on all sides of the shape and cut it out of the plastic at the same time, remove the pattern from underneath the plastic and place the plastic on your cutting mat. Now align the ¼″ line of the ruler you usually rotary cut with so it travels through the center of 2 dots along 1 line on the

plastic. Position the Touch Knife or X-ACTO knife next to the ruler's edge and score the plastic. There is no need to press hard—just score the plastic, beginning and ending well beyond the dots. Repeat this process for all lines and dots. You might want to sacrifice a template to practice and get the feel of this method if it is new to you. Score all sides of the shape. Once the plastic is scored adequately it will crack off precisely, resulting in an extremely accurate template that includes a ¼″ seam allowance on all sides of the shape. Making templates this way ensures that your template shapes include the exact same seam allowance as your rotary-cut shapes. If tips need to be trimmed, I do that at this time.

4. In patchwork we often have shapes that, once the seam allowance has been added, have extended points or tips, such as on diamonds, triangles, and so on. You can remove these points on the template shape in one of two ways.

Trimming Tips and Extended Points

Method 1: If you are working with 45° shapes, such as diamonds or half-square triangles, you can double-blunt the tip, which eliminates the excess and allows those shapes to align with square edges. You can use this technique on any extended points, although they may not always align with their sewing partners. To double-blunt extended tips, trim ¼″ from the dot at a right angle from both lines that extend from the dot. This means you will be making 2 cuts.

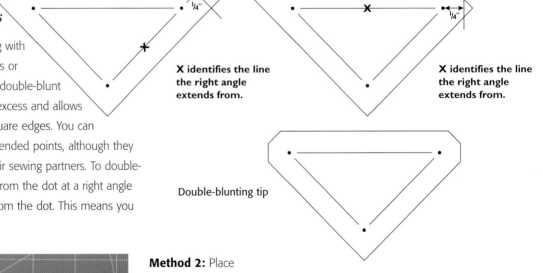

X identifies the line the right angle extends from.

X identifies the line the right angle extends from.

Double-blunting tip

Method 2: Place the template with the extended points under the shape it gets sewn to and trim the points off.

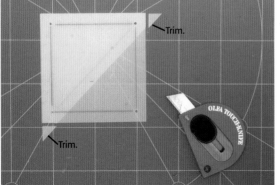

Trimming points, Method 2

5. Punch holes exactly over the dots, using a $\frac{1}{16}''$ hole punch, or place the template face down on a towel and carefully pierce the plastic at the dot with a stiletto or large needle by gently twisting, taking care not to crack the plastic. The hole should only be large enough to insert a pencil or marking tool and make a mark on the fabric.

6. Before using the templates to cut fabric, place the templates over the pattern to be sure the dots appear through your punched holes. Then place the appropriate template shapes onto one another as if you were sewing. Because the template shapes interrelate to each other, the edges and holes should line up exactly. Do not cut fabric until your templates are accurate. If they do not line up in plastic, they will not line up in fabric.

Noteworthy

Make a simple right-angle triangle template, double-blunt the extended tips, and punch holes at the dots. This now becomes a tool that you can use to trim points from rotary-cut right-angle triangles, and you can use the corner to make $\frac{1}{4}''$ marks on fabric when needed. This template application will be used in the *Fire Fly* and *Lotus Flower* projects using one of the project's templates.

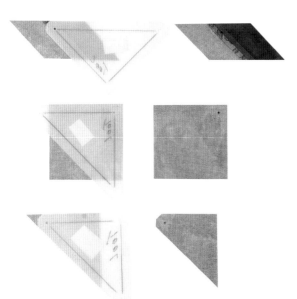

Template placement for making $\frac{1}{4}''$ mark using template as a tool when needed

CUTTING FABRIC WITH TEMPLATES

Noteworthy

If there is a discrepancy between fabric grain and fabric print, cut with the fabric print to please the eye.

1. Place each template face down on the wrong side of the fabric. Reverse templates will be placed right side up.

2. If appropriate, cut a strip of fabric a little wider than the template so you are not encumbered by a lot of fabric when cutting with the template.

3. To prevent the templates from sliding and slipping on the fabric when you are cutting, cut small pieces of masking or painter's tape and roll it so it has double-stick capability and place it on the right side of the template.

4. With an appropriate fabric marker, make dots through the punched holes onto the fabric.

5. Trim off the excess strip fabric. Holding the 18mm (my favorite) or 28mm rotary cutter like a pencil, cut the fabric around the template, keeping the blade next to the edge of the plastic template. Use the Olfa 12″ × 12″ square revolving mat to do this so you can easily turn your work and cut comfortably. To avoid shaving your template edge, do not lift the cutter off the mat until you have completed cutting each edge. Even if you must stop to rearrange your hands on a long edge, leave the cutter blade on the mat. Lifting the cutter up and down is what shaves the template edge.

Cutting fabric using a template and a small rotary cutter, as described, is the only time I can sit and rotary cut with total accuracy.

Cutting fabric using the template

Accurate Sewing

Noteworthy

Before you begin to sew, be sure your machine is clean and in good working order, have a new needle in place, sit in front of your machine, and have good light. My husband thinks I could land planes in my sewing room, but I've added something new that has become invaluable to me. When I sew, I am constantly watching the side of the foot to be sure my fabric is positioned correctly under the foot, which ensures my ¼″ seam allowance. To light that area I take my Ott-Lite (the one that opens like an L), open it up, lay it on its side, and position it on my acrylic table so that the light shines directly on the side of the foot. This is the area that I need to clearly see, and placing the light as described has made a huge difference for me.

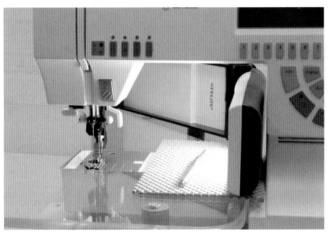

Ott-Lite illuminating side of sewing foot

Using ¼″ seam allowances (the exact same seam allowance you have allowed for in your cutting) ensures successful patchwork piecing. Remember, in order to have all the cut pieces sew back together like a puzzle, you must take off an accurate ¼″ seam on all sides of all pieces—no more and no less.

All machines are different. You must find out how to achieve a ¼″ seam allowance on your machine before you begin to sew. A ¼″ seam allowance is not a personal issue; it is a mathematical one. Some options to achieve a ¼″ seam allowance are to use tape, a magnetic seam guide, or a ¼″ foot, or to move the needle position.

Whatever method you use, check it for accuracy before you begin sewing. One way to check for accuracy is to cut 2 strips 1″ × 3½″ of any fabric, pair them right sides

together with edges even and aligned, and sew down the length with an accurate ¼″ seam allowance (use a large stitch length in case you need to remove the stitches and retest). Open the 2-strip unit and press the seam allowance to one side. This unit should now measure 1½″ from edge to edge and also ¾″ from the seam to the edge in both directions.

If it does, your cutting and sewing are accurate. If it does not measure correctly, either your cutting or sewing or both are in question, and you need to make the appropriate adjustment. Even if you are just a little bit off, your work will reflect the inaccuracy. For example, let's say you are sewing a 6″ Bear's Paw block that has 45 pieces and numerous seams and you want to join it to a 6″ Snowball block that has only 5 pieces and 4 seams. If you are just a little bit off, these 2 blocks will never be the same size because the accumulation of the "little bit off" will be greater in the block with more pieces and seams than in the other. You must establish and maintain an accurate ¼″ seam allowance. Additionally, the more pieces in the block and/or the smaller the block, the more crucial accuracy becomes and the less tolerance for error exists.

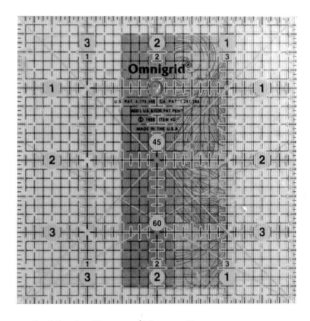

One method for checking your ¼″ seam allowance

SEWING STRAIGHT / CHAIN PIECING

This is the most overlooked area of accurate, precise sewing. If poorly executed, this one skill creates more problems than any other. The ability to sew straight—that is, to enter onto the fabric at ¼″, stay at ¼″, and exit off the fabric at ¼″—is crucial to quality workmanship.

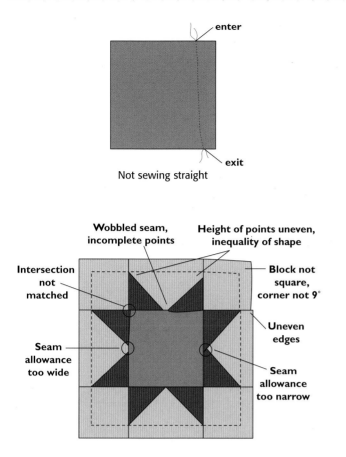

Not sewing straight

Some problems associated with not sewing straight

1. Be sure the pieces or rows or units you are sewing are positioned on each other correctly. Sit directly in front of your needle, clearly see your sewing path, and make sure you have a sense of squareness or straightness. Look at the lines on your throat plate or the edge of your machine; as you place your fabric under the needle, the edge you are sewing should be perpendicular to the front edge of your machine. Begin to develop this sense as you continue to sew.

2. Most of us chain piece by pushing our fabric pieces under the front of the foot. This not only prevents us from getting onto our fabric at exactly ¼″ because we are at least ½″ away from the needle but also skews or shifts the two pieces of fabric being sewn because the foot pushes the top layer as the feed dogs grab only the bottom piece. To remedy this, rather than pushing the pieces under the front of the foot, slightly lift the presser foot (do not raise it all the way up and disengage it), position the work under the foot so the fabric edge touches the front of the needle, align the right edge of the fabric with the ¼″ seam guide, and lower the foot.

3. Sew slowly; be sure you can clearly see the sewing path and the needle enter and exit the fabric exactly where you want it to. Carefully guide your work from the left as it goes under the needle, while using a stiletto or something similar to help keep the raw edge of your fabric pieces against or next to whatever seam guide you are using. Sew until the needle is off the fabric and in the machine, keeping the corner of the work against the seam guide so the feed dogs cannot pull the corner to the left. This keeps the fabric from shifting and ensures straight sewing by making sure that you enter onto and exit off the fabric at ¼″.

4. Sew for a short distance with no fabric under the presser foot—just do not lift the presser foot. It is not a race; do not concern yourself with anything else until the sewing needle is completely off the fabric edge of the pieces you are sewing. Then, stop your machine, get the next 2 pieces to be sewn, position them appropriately, and begin sewing again.

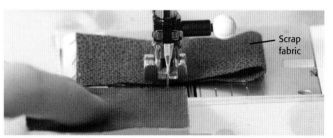

Lift the foot slightly and move the fabric under the foot so the fabric touches the needle and the right edge is in position for ¼″ sewing.

Sewing Even Edges

When sewing two pieces of fabric together, it is important that their edges are even and aligned. If one edge moves away from the other, you will not be taking the accurate ¼″ seam allowance off both edges, even if you have cut accurately and sewn with an exact ¼″ seam allowance. This can happen very easily. Usually it is the edge of the bottom piece that moves away from the edge of the top piece, which is the one we look at when we sew. Always be sure the edges are aligned and even before sewing.

Measuring Your Patchwork

Measuring will enable you to monitor and maintain accuracy and identify what seams need to be adjusted. Refer to page 34 for specifics on measuring and page 31 if using templates to monitor your work.

Stitch Length

After testing for an accurate ¼″ seam allowance with the two-strip technique (page 34), I adjust the stitch length to approximately 15–20 stitches per inch. You want to be sure the length is not so small that it gathers up the fabric or becomes difficult to remove the stitches if necessary.

I often change the stitch length depending on what I'm doing. When I'm experimenting or if I'm unsure about matching a heavily seamed intersection, I increase the stitch length so I can easily remove the stitches and re-sew if necessary. Another situation in which I slightly increase the stitch length is when I am sewing a bulky or heavily seamed area, because it tends to makes the seam suppler rather than rigid and stiff. I decrease the stitch length as I approach dots when doing Y-seam construction (page 46), which enables me to sew very close to the appropriate dots without sewing into them. I also decrease my stitch length if the seam will be pressed open, which creates an opportunity for thread to show.

Sewing Thread Type and Color

I use 100% cotton DMC Machine Embroidery Thread 50/2 (50-weight/2-ply) in the top and bobbin of my machine for all my piecing. This is a fine, thin, left-twist, long-staple thread that takes up less space, resulting in flatter seams. This thread also leaves no fluff under the throat plate and allows you to significantly increase the amount of thread on the bobbin.

I use a medium muddy tan or gray color, which blends in with most fabrics. Matching color is not as important as blending or camouflaging. You do not want to see the thread from the right side of the work. When in doubt, choose a darker thread in relation to the fabric. If I were working in black and white, for instance, I would choose black thread. When there are open seams or when numerous seams intersect, that creates more opportunity for thread to show, so be attentive to thread color and stitch length.

Noteworthy

Even when I think I'm being careful, there are times when I can see little dots of light thread showing from the right side of my block. When this happens, I gently, precisely, and carefully graze the thread with the lead of a pencil, which takes away the lightness, making it less noticeable to the eye. It is tempting to use a permanent marker but I always try the pencil first. If that does not do the trick, then and only then do I use a permanent marker to "custom dye" the thread. Be sure the marker is on the dry side instead of the wet to prevent any bleeding to other areas of your work.

Feeding Fabric Under the Needle Smoothly

Sew on a folded scrap piece of fabric first, sewing off its edge so the needle is in the machine, then feed or chain piece (page 34) your "real" pieces behind the scrap. When you have fed all your pieces under the needle, stop your machine with the needle down into the machine, but do not lift the presser foot. Cut off your scrap piece, bring it to the front of the foot, sew on the scrap piece again, and cut off your real pieces.

As a result, you are not pulling your work out from the machine to clip threads, which leaves little thread tails all over the back of your block or quilt and at the ends of seams. There are also no threads on the floor, resulting in a neater work area. Whenever you sew from edge to edge, your machine will take on fabric pieces much easier if it is already engaged in sewing, as on the scrap. If you are doing Y-seam construction or if you do not use a scrap to begin and end your sewing, you will need to hold the top and bobbin threads when you begin sewing or you will get a bobbin bulge on the back of your work. If this happens, remove the threads and begin again.

Noteworthy

I have been asked why I do not use two scrap pieces, one to begin with and one to end with. When I tried using two, I was always looking for the second scrap. When you work with only one scrap piece you always know where it is!

Use a stiletto as an extension of your hand to help guide pieces of fabric under the needle straight and to keep their edges against or aligned with whatever seam guide you are using. Or, use a wooden skewer, toothpick, seam ripper, or large pin.

A straight-stitch throat plate (the one with the tiny round hole) is a must for smooth, straight stitching and creates less opportunity for fabric to be pulled down into the machine. It is also a must when machine quilting because it will result in straighter stitches. For obvious reasons the needle must be kept in the center position when using the straight-stitch throat plate. The zigzag throat plate has a larger opening for fabric to go down into.

Change your sewing machine needle after six to eight hours of sewing. Clean under the throat plate and oil after every fifteen to twenty hours of sewing, or at least after completing each project. You'll be grateful for how well your machine will perform if you treat it with kindness. If you have a dull or burred needle and a zigzag throat plate on, the needle will grab the fabric and pull it into the machine.

Removing Stitches

When it becomes necessary to remove stitches and re-sew, do so carefully so as not to distress, tear, or fray your fabric. The seam ripper is an invaluable, helpful, and important tool but should be used carefully, properly, and with respect. Never "rip" out stitches. Instead, when you have a line of stitches that need to be released, cut every third or fourth stitch, turn your work over, and lift that thread. It will easily release, and the two pieces will separate. Careful removal of inappropriate stitches will enable you to reposition and re-sew over and over (if necessary) without having to dispose of the pieces and re-cut.

PINNING

I use 1¼″-long IBC Super Fine Silk Pins #5004 that are .5mm. They are long, fine, thin pins without glass heads. I also use Clover Patchwork Pin (Fine) that are .4mm, which is 20% finer than .5mm pins. These are very thin and delicate—not for securing heavily seamed intersections but for pinning two fabrics together. Both pins slide into fabric easily, with little or no distortion on the edge of the fabric, which results in a flatter edge for the machine to sew over. I sew over all my pins successfully without breaking needles or harming my machine because the combination of slow sewing and fine pins allows the machine needle to slide in front of or behind the pins as it sews. Speed is what breaks sewing machine needles.

I use pins to secure intersections, match points (alignment pin), ease areas of fullness, keep outside edges even,

and match dots, which helps position one piece onto another properly and aids in Y-seam construction. I use pins whenever it helps my work and benefits my sewing.

I usually position the pinheads to the left, which creates a flat, smooth path for the sewing machine to follow.

My preferred pin placement

When sewing strips of fabric together, or when adding borders onto quilts or sashing onto blocks, place the pins parallel to the edge and remove them as you approach them. This creates much less distortion than perpendicular pin placement does.

Parallel pin placement for strips and borders

PRESSING SEAMS

Effective pressing is setting a seam with heat, not pressure or weight. Use a hot, dry iron and lift and place the iron onto the appropriate areas to be pressed instead of sliding the iron around. Steam dampens the fabric, which can stretch, distort, pleat, and pucker it. If I have an unruly or bulky seam I sometimes custom dampen the area by dipping my finger into a small bowl of water kept at the ironing board and specifically dampen only that area, then press it with the dry iron. Move the iron in the direction of the fabric grain instead of at an angle to prevent any distortion.

Before pressing a seam allowance, set the seam by placing the iron on the stitching line just sewn. This relaxes the thread, eases in any fullness, and nestles the stitches into the fabric, so they become one. You will find that if you do this, your work will be flatter, smoother, squarer, and more accurate. Setting the seam or opening a seam is the only time I press from the wrong side of the fabric.

I press seams all to one side, or sometimes open, and occasionally I collapse them. Ideally, you want to plan and create opposing seams to aid in the matching of intersections and in maintaining squareness. If a seam allowance needs to be redirected, you must first re-set the seam as discussed earlier, then press it in the new direction.

Pieces will also fit together much easier if each seam is pressed before it is sewn over, and pressing each seam will help give you the most precise measurement. I use my hands and fingers to arrange, manipulate, and prepare the area to be pressed and then place the iron in that area. If you have cut and sewn accurately, there is no need to smooth and stretch the fabric outward toward the edges.

Pressing can either distort your work or help you shape it. The direction seam allowances are pressed can also make a difference in how the piecing looks from the right side of the block. Pressing seams in one direction could round out a point in some instances, while pressing in the opposite direction could sharpen the point—or opening a seam could improve it even more and distribute the bulk. Poor pressing can distort beautiful piecing.

When opening a seam, an alternative to setting the seam with the iron is to first open the seam with your hands by running a fingernail down the seam while supporting it with the opposite hand. When you do this you will feel the two fabrics separate and the stitches relax. A good open seam requires the two fabrics to separate down to the thread. After opening the seam with your hands, use the iron to press from the back first and then from the right side.

There are times, in pressing a long seam of multiple intersections, when areas of the seam allowance do not want to press in the direction you choose, and forcing them creates lumps because the fabric will always be trying to go in the other direction. This happens, for instance, when you are sewing pieced blocks to plain fabric alternate blocks. The seam allowance will always naturally fall in the direction of least resistance, in this case toward the plain fabric alternate block. When this struggle occurs, I snip into the seam allowance (not the stitching) at the intersection area, which releases the seam allowance to redirect itself. You can hear it say thank you.

The result is that over the long seam, the seam allowance goes back and forth, always toward the side of least resistance, and the seam from the right side of the quilt is straight and flat. A good illustration of this is on page 63 in the *French Confection* project. Use this technique whenever the circumstance arises on display work.

Noteworthy

Collapsing seams helps to distribute and reduce bulk and can be done on simple four-seam intersections. To collapse a seam, remove (do not cut) the vertical stitches in the seam allowance at the intersection, one at a time, to the last horizontal line of stitching on both pieces. With your hands arrange or "collapse" the seam allowance in opposite directions and press.

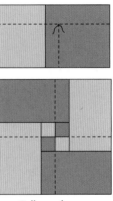

Collapsed seam

BLOCKING

Carefully blocking units, rows, or blocks brings them to their appropriate size and shape if there is a slight discrepancy. Remember, fabric is fluid, and quality cotton is forgiving and can be arranged and manipulated, if necessary. During the sewing process it is important that units and rows maintain their correct grid dimension and shape.

To block a row or unit, I press it, place a ruler over the piece, and measure and evaluate its shape, and then rearrange if appropriate (if only a slight adjustment needs to be made). I pin it in place if necessary, place the ruler over it again, weight it with a book, and let it cool in place before moving it.

Take care to maintain a sense of squareness throughout the sewing process. Misshapen units and rows will create misshapen blocks.

To block a completed block, cut a piece of freezer paper larger than the unfinished size of your block and iron it to your ironing-board cover. Now draw the size of square you need, including seam allowances. Freezer paper shrinks somewhat, so press it in place first, then draw the square to ensure accuracy. Draw a line from corner to corner in both directions to identify the center, place a pin through the center of the block, and place the block on the drawn square. Lightly dampen the block and gently encourage the edges outward to meet the drawn guidelines, or pat and scooch (technical terms) the edges inward to meet them. Pin the block in place and press it carefully, then put a square ruler on top of the block, place a book or weight on it, and let it cool before moving it. Final pressing from the top (for pieced blocks) on a soft towel allows the seam allowances to sink into the towel for a flatter look and eliminates the possibility of ridges forming from the seam allowances.

TRIMMING AND GRADING SEAM ALLOWANCES

The projects in this book all use a ¼″ seam allowance. Some of the piecing is intricate and very small, so trimming seams will alleviate and distribute the accumulation of bulk. Trim seams to a generous ⅛″ whether the seam is open or pressed in one direction. If the seam is pressed open, trim one side and then the other. It is much easier to trim an open seam than it is to open an already trimmed seam. I trim seams with scissors because by the time you arrange your work on your rotary mat, position the ruler correctly, and trim with the rotary cutter you could have trimmed with scissors. Creating well-sewn, flat, intricate piecing will require trimmed seam allowances.

Grading seams is also an option anytime and is preferred when you have a heavily seamed intersection. Grading creates a slope rather than a short step (like that created by a trimmed seam) and results in a flatter intersection. To grade a seam you will be looking at the wrong side of the work. Trim the seam allowance that is on top and closest to you more than the seam allowance underneath. Some sewers know how to slant their scissors and grade a seam in one cut. I do not know how to do that and therefore must make two cuts, which takes twice the time. I trim or grade small work because it eliminates bulk and makes quilting easier, but you may find that larger blocks do not need it. It often depends on the purpose of the quilt and the size of the pieces. Small work demands trimmed or graded seams to lie flat and view

well. Always press first, then trim or grade, so scissors are the best tool to use. Follow these guidelines:

- Use serrated-edge scissors, which grab the fabric rather than letting it slip and slide over the scissor blade's edge, resulting in miscutting.

- Do not trim or grade too much because the seam allowance will stand straight up rather than press to one side or the other. This condition creates problems during quilting because the seam allowance wiggles from one side of the seam to the other.

- You must also know that your work is correct before trimming it. If you trim or grade a seam and then discover that you need to remove stitches and re-sew, your seam allowance will have been distorted and changed, which makes re-sewing a little more difficult. This is just one of the many reasons why it is so important to maintain grid dimension and to critique and correct your work before trimming or grading. If you do trim and then discover that you need to remove stitches and re-sew, you can remove the stitches and measure over from the opposite edge the grid dimension plus ¼″ and draw a sewing line. If you are using templates and have dots on your fabric, just connect the dots to create your sewing line.

- Do not trim seams until you are ready to sew over them with the next seam. That way you leave the door open for change and correction as long as possible.

- When your quilt or block is complete, it should have a ¼″ seam allowance on all sides. Trimming up or squaring up is not a way to correct problems or to bring your work to the right size. Trimming up should only create straight edges and remove thread tails.

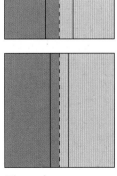

Trimmed   Graded   Trimmed

Construction Techniques

There are always many roads that lead to the same place. This is also true of sewing techniques and methods available to accomplish a specific sewing task. The techniques and methods described here work for me and are based on precision, accuracy, and efficiency, as well as the type of specific task. I remain open to new techniques but never compromise or sacrifice accuracy for speed. Sometimes fast, quick, easy construction techniques actually take more time than more traditional techniques and limit your color, fabric, and creative choices and ability to compose and create custom work. I encourage you to explore, experience, experiment, and evaluate new techniques and then make your own choices based on the task at hand.

Oversize and Custom-Cut Technique

This technique is self-explanatory. A pieced unit is created deliberately larger than needed and then the exact or required size unit is cut from it. This technique can be implemented for a variety of types of pieced units, including half-square triangle units, quarter-square triangle units, some pieced 45° diamond units, and four-patches, to name a few. The reason I oversize and custom cut whenever I can is because, in my experience, when I make pieced units actual size they never really turn out the exact size they should and they are not perfectly square. If you begin with inferior units you are already at a disadvantage and you haven't even begun to assemble your quilt or block yet. The advantages of this technique are that it is stress-free, the required size unit is cut exactly and precisely, and the seam allowances are pressed and trimmed. I always oversize and custom cut in any scale, whenever I can, because it gives me better work. When you oversize, always follow the actual mathematical formula first, and THEN add an additional ½″ or so and cut. In my opinion the improved results far outweigh the extra time it takes.

For example, let's say I want to create a 1″ finished half-square triangle unit. Rather than cutting a 1⅞″ × 1⅞″ square (finished size plus ⅞″) of two fabrics, cutting them in half diagonally, and sewing two of the triangles back together to result in a 1½″ half-square triangle unit (1″ plus seam allowance), I increase the size of the 1⅞″ × 1⅞″ square to perhaps 2⅜″ × 2⅜″. The increase I

use is ½″, although there is no specific formula—just larger. The unit can then be custom cut in the exact desired size from the larger square. How to accurately custom cut an exact-sized unit from an oversized unit will be explained as each type of unit is introduced.

Half-Square Triangle Units

Individual triangles and half-square triangle units for the projects in this book are created in several different ways, depending on their size and on how many are needed of a particular fabric. I have specified which method I felt was the most successful in each individual case, but you always have the option of choosing your own.

I create half-square triangle units in a variety of ways: individual half-square triangles (my favorite), stitched grid, and square-to-square. Individual half-square or right-angle triangles are a common shape used in patchwork and are simply created by cutting a square in half diagonally, which results in the two short sides of the triangles being on the straight grain and the one longer leg being on the bias grain. Two of these triangles sewn together create a square.

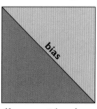

Half-square triangle unit

INDIVIDUAL HALF-SQUARE TRIANGLES
Cutting

1. To cut individual half-square triangles that include a ¼″ seam allowance, determine the finished length of the short side of the triangle needed and add ⅞″ to that number. If oversizing and custom cutting this unit, after adding ⅞″ add an additional ½″ to the cut square and refer to Square-to-Square Technique (page 42) for instructions on how to custom cut the exact-sized unit from the oversized unit.

2. Cut a square that size.

3. Place the edge of the ruler on the square, exactly corner to corner, and cut. The blade does not take up space so there is no need to back up the ruler edge to

accommodate the blade. Another option is to first position the cutter blade where you want to begin cutting, then move the ruler next to the cutter blade. Whichever method you choose, be accurate.

Sewing

1. To sew individual triangles together to form a square (half-square triangle unit), pair 2 triangles, right sides together, aligning all 3 edges.

2. Sew down the long bias edge. To maintain an accurate ¼″ seam allowance from point to point and be able to chain piece, lift the presser foot slightly, move the paired triangles under the foot and up to the needle, lower the foot, and sew, stopping when the needle is off the fabric and in the machine; continue to feed each pair of triangles similarly. The points will overlap and you will not have any bent points or points shoved into the machine. Refer to Chain Piecing (page 34).

3. Separate the chain of triangles by snipping the threads between the units.

4. Trimming dog ears before pressing will create a squarer half-square triangle unit. Press the stitches, trim off the dog-ears (the excess that extends beyond the end of the seam), and then open the piece for final pressing. I open the seam on half-square triangles 1½″ or smaller.

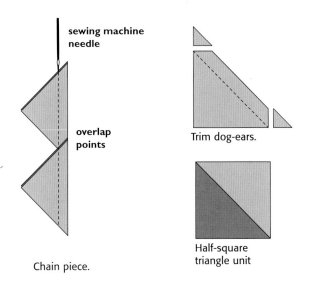

Chain piece.

Trim dog-ears.

Half-square triangle unit

STITCHED-GRID TECHNIQUE

This technique is based on the "add ⅞″ to the finished size of the half-square triangle units" premise. I use this technique sparingly when I need a few units from the same two fabrics, since this technique yields eight half-square triangle units.

1. Determine the finished size of the desired half-square triangle unit.

2. Add ⅞″ to this number and then double it (e.g., 1″ finished unit + ⅞″ = 1⅞″ × 2 = 3¾″ × 3¾″ square). You have the option of implementing the oversize and custom-cut technique by increasing the size of the 2 original cut squares by 1″, proceeding as stated, and then custom cutting the exact size desired from the oversized units. See Square-to-Square Technique (page 42) for how to custom cut.

3. Cut a 3¾″ × 3¾″ square from each of the 2 desired fabrics. Place them right sides together and draw lines on the lighter fabric from corner to corner in both directions and horizontally and vertically. These drawn lines are eventual cutting lines.

4. Sew ¼″ on both sides of the diagonal lines only.

5. Cut on all drawn lines to yield 8 segments.

6. Trim the dog-ears, press the seams open, and trim seams. Each unit will measure 1½″ × 1½″ square if you have cut and sewn accurately.

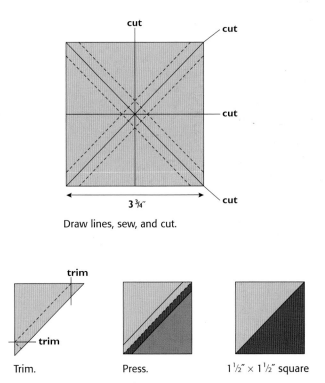

Draw lines, sew, and cut.

Trim.

Press.

1½″ × 1½″ square

SQUARE-TO-SQUARE TECHNIQUE

This technique creates individual half-square triangle units and is successful, simple, and accurate. I use this technique when I need only one or two units each from a variety of fabrics and colors, as in the *Fire Fly* project (page 67).

Let's say you want to create a 1″ finished half-square triangle unit.

1. Cut 2 squares 1½″ × 1½″ of 2 chosen fabrics. To oversize, cut squares 2″ × 2″.

2. Draw a diagonal line on the wrong side of the lightest fabric.

3. Pair both squares, right sides together, and sew on this line.

4. Trim to within ¼″ of the stitches, press the seam open, and trim seams again to a generous ⅛″. If you are making larger units, press the seam allowance to one side.

5. The unit is now 1½″ × 1½″ square.

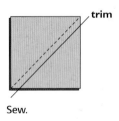
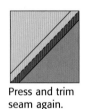

trim

Sew.

Press and trim seam again.

6. If your unit is oversized, custom cut the desired unit from it using a square ruler with a 45° line, as illustrated.

7. Position the ruler on the oversized square so that the 45° line is on the seam and there is fabric visible beyond the 1½″ lines on all 4 sides. Trim the first 2 sides.

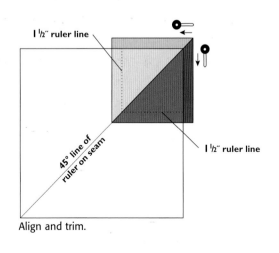

1½″ ruler line

45° line of ruler on seam

1½″ ruler line

Align and trim.

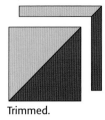

Trimmed.

8. Rotate one half turn and trim the other 2 sides.

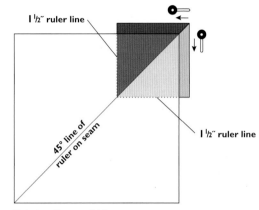

1½″ ruler line

45° line of ruler on seam

1½″ ruler line

Rotate, align, and trim.

1½″ × 1½″ square

Noteworthy

Rather than rolling the cutter to the corner toward the seam and bulk and risking that the fabric might move under the ruler, first cut the corner by pressing down with the cutter, then pull toward yourself or reposition the cutter and roll toward the corner, then cut the top edge.

STICKY-NOTE TECHNIQUE

When you have many half-square triangles and are using the square-to-square and oversize and custom-cut techniques as in the *Fire Fly* project (page 67), you can eliminate the need to draw a sewing line. Only use this technique when oversizing.

1. Position the sticky edge of a sticky note on your machine, lining it up with the center of the needle outward toward you. Use a ruler to be sure it is straight and square. Do not cover the feed dogs.

2. Align the paired squares to be sewn diagonally, so both their opposite corner points are always on the edge of the sticky note. This will ensure that you are sewing diagonally from one corner to the other.

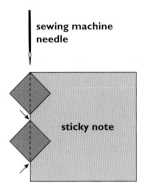

sewing machine needle

sticky note

3. See Square-to-Square Technique (page 42) for instructions on how to custom cut.

Quarter-Square Triangle Units

These units are created by cutting squares of fabric into quarters diagonally, which places the straight of grain on the longest side of the triangle, and then sewing those triangles back together to create a square. These units can be oversized and custom cut (page 44).

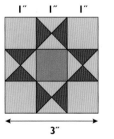

Quarter-square triangle unit

1″ 1″ 1″

3″

To know what size to cut the squares, first determine the finished length of the longest side of the triangle and add 1¼″. For example, if the finished length of the long leg of the triangle is 1″, then 1″ + 1¼″ = 2¼″ × 2¼″ square.

Cutting the 2¼″ × 2¼″ square into quarters is a simple task but it must be done accurately to maintain equality among the shapes.

1. Place your ruler edge diagonally on the square, exactly through both corners. Firmly stabilize the ruler with your hands so it does not move while you are cutting.

2. Cut with your rotary cutter angled slightly, so the blade cuts where the ruler and fabric meet.

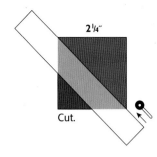

2¼″

Cut.

3. Carefully lift the ruler and reposition its edge through the 2 opposite corners, and cut without disturbing the pieces.

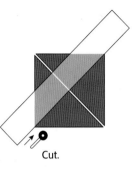

Cut.

If the triangles move when you reposition the ruler, you can cut them one at a time. Take your square or long ruler and position it on the individual triangle so that the top edge of the ruler, or a horizontal line, is on the top edge of the triangle and the side edge of the ruler is aligned vertically from the top edge and through the point.

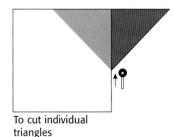

To cut individual triangles

Sewing quarter-square triangle units is not difficult, but if you sew the wrong edges together you can get the color out of position. If you follow these simple steps, you will always have the units sewn together correctly.

1. Lay out the unit(s) and think of the 4 triangle positions as north, south, east, and west. Always sew east to south (which leaves north and west; no need to remember). Always sew with east and west on top, from the corner to the point. Always press to east and west, keeping the iron away from the bias edges.

2. Join east/south to north/west, pinning at the intersection and each end. Press this seam open.

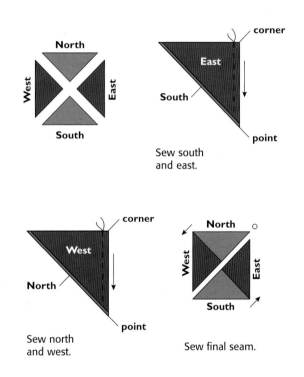

Sew south and east.

Sew north and west.

Sew final seam.

3. When custom cutting oversized units, you must work from the center intersection out toward all 4 edges one-half the cut size.

This is easier to do if the cut size of the unit is divisible by 2. If it is not, make a square from template plastic the cut size needed, draw lines from corner to corner in both directions, place the template on the larger unit (aligning the center intersection and diagonal lines of the template over the seamlines and intersection of the pieced unit), and custom cut.

For example, to custom cut a 1½″ × 1½″ square from a larger quarter-square triangle unit, position the square ruler so that the ¾″ (half of 1½″) intersection of the ruler is on the center intersection of the unit, which places the

corner of the ruler where the 2 different fabrics join, and the 45° line on 1 diagonal seam. At the same time be sure the other diagonal seam runs corner to corner through the ⅛″ grid squares on the ruler.

4. When all 3 alignment perspectives are in place, cut the side and top edges.

5. Rotate the segment, reposition the square ruler again, and make the final 2 cuts. It is important to align the ruler as described to create equality among the 4 triangles and have the seams split the 4 corners exactly.

Noteworthy

Rather than rolling the cutter to the corner toward the seam and bulk and risking that the fabric might move under the ruler, first cut the corner by pressing down with the cutter, then pull toward yourself or reposition the cutter and roll toward the cut corner, then cut the top edge.

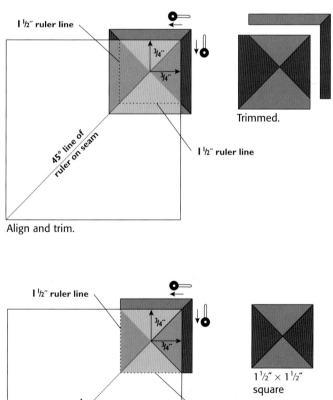

Align and trim.

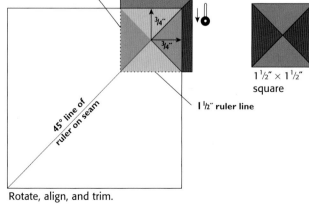

Rotate, align, and trim.

Sew-and-Flip Technique

This technique is used to create a variety of shapes, including double half-square triangle units and square-in-a-square units. It eliminates cutting triangles and sewing exposed bias and uses squares and rectangles instead to create the triangles.

DOUBLE HALF-SQUARE TRIANGLES

Although this unit is composed of 3 triangles, it will be constructed using a rectangle and 2 squares. Speaking in finished-size dimensions, the rectangle is always twice as long as it is high, and the squares are the same size as the height of the rectangle. To cut fabric and sew you need to add ¼" seam allowance to all sides of each shape.

This unit is often called a Flying Geese unit and can also be used to create star points or a parallelogram, depending on the direction of the second diagonal seam. I first became aware of this sew-and-flip technique from the book *Quilts! Quilts! Quilts!!!* by Diana McClun and Laura Nownes. Although I construct this unit a little differently, it is credited to them. I use this same technique when making a Square-in-a-Square unit.

Flying Geese
unit

Star Point unit

Parallelogram

1. Cut a rectangle and 2 squares.

2. Draw a diagonal line on the wrong side of each square.

3. Place 1 square onto 1 end of the rectangle, right sides together, being sure all appropriate edges are aligned, and sew just on the scrap side of the line. (The scrap side is the side that gets trimmed away). My experience with this technique has been that if I sew directly on the line, the square's corner does not meet the rectangle's corner exactly. Also, thread takes up space, so sewing on the scrap side of the line gives a small amount of space back and makes the 2 corners meet more comfortably.

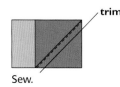

trim

Sew.

4. Bring the square's corner over the stitching to the rectangle's corner. If the corners meet comfortably and to your standards, press and trim only the square's scrap triangle to within ⅛" of the stitches, leaving the rectangle in place. Do not use the iron to swoop the triangle over the stitching to the opposite corner; you must place it and press. I do this because if the square's corner gets pressed beyond the rectangle's corner, it's tempting to trim off the excess, which changes the size of the triangle, or if you leave it the unit is now incorrect. If you place the square's and rectangle's corners on top of each other and press, even if the fold is not exactly at the stitching line it will not matter.

Trim.

Press.

5. Add the second square at the other end and sew as described in Steps 3 and 4, except begin sewing from the bottom edge up to the corner, which will create a straight rather than rounded bottom edge. The direction of the second diagonal could change, depending on what kind of unit you are making.

trim

Sew from the
bottom edge to
the corner.

Trim.

Press.

Noteworthy

Leave the rectangle (or large square in the case of the Square-in-a-Square unit page 46) in place as a safety-net feature in the event that the corners do not quite meet. If that happens, when you join this unit to something else you would use the rectangle's edge (or large square's edge) to align with, not the small square's edge. This does add a little bulk, but it's well worth it. This unit always remains the size of either the rectangle or the larger square you begin with.

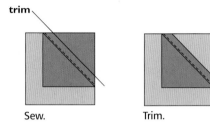

SQUARE-IN-A-SQUARE UNIT

When creating a Square-in-a-Square unit, speaking in finished measurements, the 4 small squares are half the size of the large square. For example, if the large square is 4″ × 4″, the small squares are 2″ × 2″. To cut and sew you must add a ¼″ seam allowance on all sides of each shape.

1. Place a small square onto a larger square and draw a line diagonally. Sew just on the scrap side of the line.

2. Trim only the small square's triangle (leaving the larger square in place).

trim

Sew. Trim.

3. Bring 1 corner over the stitching to meet another. Press. Notice that the larger square, which ends up holding the 4 corner triangles and becomes the square on point, remains in place.

4. Repeat Steps 1–3 to attach the 3 remaining small squares.

Press and sew. **trim** Trim. Press.

trim

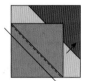

Sew. Trim. **trim** Press and sew.

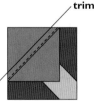

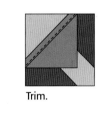

Trim. Press. **finished shape**

Y-Seam Construction

This type of seam construction is needed when three seams meet in one place, which makes it necessary to leave the seam allowances free to accomplish a flat, smooth intersection. This kind of sewing is not difficult, but you will need to remove the work from the machine and reposition it often, so just resign yourself to this slower type of sewing.

Some of the most beautiful designs require Y-seaming, such as the Lone Star in *Lotus Flower* (page 112), and usually require templates (page 31).

1. Punch holes in the templates and mark reference dots on the wrong side of your fabric pieces.

dots on wrong side

Mark dots.

2. Pin and sew as shown, backstitching at the Y-seam dots only, not at the edges. Stop sewing and backstitch just before entering the dot and you will create a successful, flat, smooth intersection every time. You must, however, stitch as close to the dot as possible (1/16″–1/32″) to not leave an obvious hole. I dial my stitch length smaller as I approach the dot but never enter the needle into the dot. Open the pieces.

begin **backstitch**

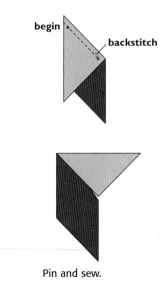

Pin and sew.

3. Pin and sew as shown, backstitching at the dot. Open the pieces.

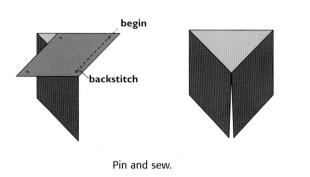

Pin and sew.

4. Sew the remaining seam. Open the pieces and press as shown.

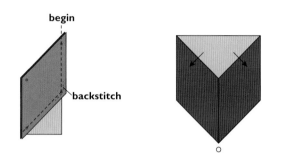

Creating Straight Strip Units

Noteworthy

The following information applies to adding borders to quilts as well.

Strip units are multiple strips sewn together. Cutting shapes from strip units is a common technique used by quiltmakers. From strips units we make nine-patches, four-patches, checkerboards, and Lone Star quilts, to name just a few. Straight, accurate, well-sewn strip units create straight lines (seams) in your quilt. The narrower the strips, the more important it is to have them be straight.

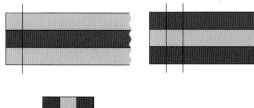

Nine-patch

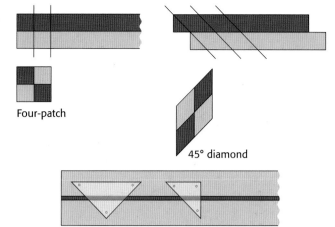

Four-patch

45° diamond

Unequal strip unit, cut using templates

Bowed or wavy seams can be caused by one or more of the following problems: cutting off grain, poor pressing, not sewing straight, and, most commonly, not keeping edges even and aligned. To help remedy these problems I sew strip units as follows.

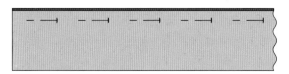

Bowed, poorly sewn, and poorly pressed strip unit

1. Cut strips accurately, straight, and on grain.

After cutting each strip, check the folds for bends or Vs. If they appear, it means the fabric is not folded on grain and needs to be refolded and the right angle re-created before cutting more strips. Strips cut on the lengthwise grain are preferred, although most quilters cut on the cross grain (I always cut borders on the length grain). Strips cut from the cross grain can be used very successfully if cut carefully.

2. Arrange the strips in the correct order to be sewn.

3. To sew the strips together, go to the ironing board with the first 2 strips to be sewn. Position the 2 strips right sides together and carefully ALIGN their correct edges exactly and carefully.

4. PRESS the 2 strips together, then PIN them together, positioning the pins parallel to the edges.

Align, press, and pin edges.

5. SEW the strips together ¼″ from the aligned, pressed, and pinned edge, slowly and carefully. Remove the pins as you sew. BE SURE YOU ARE SEWING THE CORRECT EDGES.

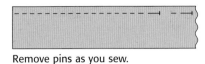

Remove pins as you sew.

6. Position the strip unit with the fabric or strip you are pressing toward FACE UP and the seam allowance toward yourself. Press the stitches. Trim the seam allowance if appropriate.

Place the strip you will press toward on top.

7. Bring the top fabric over the stitching line and finger-press, using your hands to position the fabric before pressing it with the iron. Using a hot dry iron and a short back-and-forth motion, move the iron over the seam, keeping the strip unit straight with your non-pressing hand, and PRESS the seam.

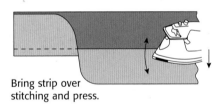

Bring strip over stitching and press.

8. If appropriate, measure the sewn strips as you sew to maintain accuracy.

Partial Seaming

This technique is used to apply borders to two project quilts, *Fire Fly* (page 67) and *Fleur-de-Lis* (page 76), although it can be used in many other scenarios. It simply means you will sew the first seam partially, instead of edge to edge, and complete the partial seam when all the other pieces that are needed have been added. The project instructions explain and illustrate this technique clearly.

Matching and Securing Points and Intersections

Successfully matching points and/or intersections requires accurate identification of the seams to be matched, careful pinning, straight sewing, and well-planned pressing.

Noteworthy

After sewing, if the points or intersection are not perfectly matched, only three things could have happened: you made a mistake in how you identified the area, how you pinned the area, or how you sewed the area. It is very easy to remove a few stitches, realign the pieces, re-pin, and re-sew. Here is where you make the choice for quality workmanship. I remove stitches and re-sew as many times as it takes to successfully accomplish the task at hand. Removing stitches and re-sewing is an important part of improving the execution of the process. You don't have to be right the first time, just the last time.

Following are specific explanations of how to match and pin common intersections and points that we often encounter in patchwork.

SIMPLE OPPOSING SEAMS, STRAIGHT OR DIAGONAL

You will encounter this type of intersection in a Four-Patch (straight) or Card Trick (diagonal) block. It simply means that at the intersection or matching area, the seam allowance on one piece is pressed to one side and its counterpart seam allowance is pressed in the opposite direction.

Align the 2 pieces to be sewn, right sides together, keeping the edges even and together. While holding the pieces together, separate the pieces at the edge only and match the intersection visually and with your hands by nesting one seam allowance tightly against the other. Now close the 2 pieces snugly and secure the area with a pin placed just to the left (¹⁄₁₆″) of the seam.

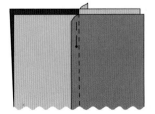

Nest seams and pin.

Four-Patch

Simple opposing straight seams

For diagonal seams, begin sewing at the seamed corner to lock in the accuracy. If the seamed corner is at the end of the seam, the sewing machine foot can drag the corner and shift the fabrics, making the unit unsquare and separating the matched intersection.

Nest seams and pin.

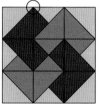

Matched intersection

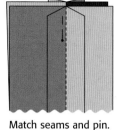

Card Trick

Simple opposing diagonal seams

Noteworthy

Ideally, you want the seam allowance that is on top pressed away from you as you sew, which means the seam allowances underneath and touching the feed dogs will remain smooth and not folded backward. When you are unable to position the work in this way, as you approach the area with the sewing machine needle, stop with the needle down, lift the fabric up, and smooth the seam allowance with a stiletto or pin.

ONE SEAM PRESSED OPEN, ONE NOT

To match this area, align the 2 pieces to be sewn, right sides together, keeping the edges even and together. While still holding the pieces together, separate them at the edge only and match the seam visually and with your hands by positioning the open seam next to the ridge created by the opposite seam allowances. Close the pieces and secure with a pin placed just to the left (¹⁄₁₆˝) of the seam.

Match seam and edges and pin.

OPEN, STRAIGHT, OR DIAGONAL SEAMS

To match this area, align the 2 pieces to be sewn, right sides together, keeping the edges even and together. While still holding the pieces together, separate them at the edge only, match the open seamlines visually, and with your hands, lay one seam onto the other exactly. Close the pieces and secure the area with a pin placed just to the left (¹⁄₁₆˝) of the seam.

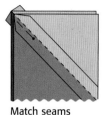

Match seams and pin.

Match seams and pin.

BOTH SEAM ALLOWANCES GOING THE SAME DIRECTION

There are times when you must match an intersection when both seam allowances are pressed in the same direction. This seam arrangement is not ideal and places all the bulk on one side. If it is unavoidable, you must stabilize and match the area for sewing.

While holding the 2 pieces right sides together, separate them at the edge only and align the seams, laying one seam onto the other. Close the area and secure with a pin placed through both seam allowances. The idea here is to compress and stabilize the bulk for sewing. The pin does not need to go down and then up through all the layers of fabric, which could create more distortion. Simply slide the pin through most layers and back up to the top, creating as flat a piece as possible. When you are sewing, the seam allowances should be positioned toward the needle; use the stiletto to press on the seam allowances and compress the bulk (kind of creating a groove to sew in). Sew slowly through the area. You may even need to use the handwheel and "walk" the needle through the bulky area.

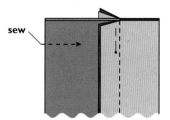

sew

Match seams and pin.

MATCHING OPEN OR OPPOSING STRAIGHT AND DIAGONAL MULTIPLE SEAMS

Some blocks create both open and opposing straight and diagonal seams at one intersection: Ohio Star, Rising Star and Square, and Dutchman's Puzzle, to name a few. To match this type of intersection, hold the 2 pieces right sides together, keeping the edges even and together. While

Ohio Star

still holding the pieces together, separate them at the edge only and you will see the 2 points that need to match exactly. Lay one point onto the other exactly, close the 2 pieces, and secure the intersection with a pin placed just to the left (¹⁄₁₆″) of the seam.

Rising Star and Square

Separate at edge only.

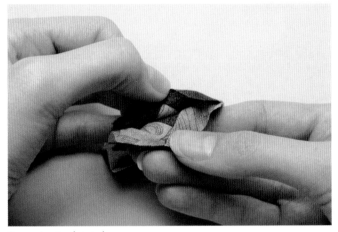

Separate at edge only.

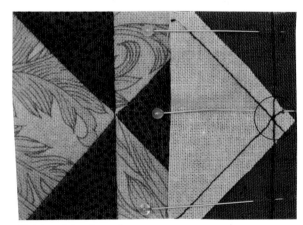

Match points, pin, and sew.

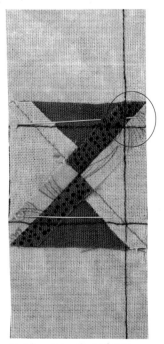

Match points, pin and sew.

Dutchman's Puzzle

Separate at edge only.

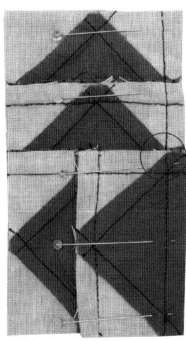

Match points, pin and sew.

ALIGNMENT PIN

To match any seams or intersections that I do not have success matching visually and with my hands as described above, I use the alignment-pin technique. This technique is always an option and can be used in any and all instances in which 2 or more seams need to match at 1 point. The pin precisely aligns 1 point or seam with another; it does not secure the area for sewing. The alignment pin is eventually removed, but it is necessary to match the 2 points and to keep them aligned on top of each other.

1. To match 2 points, place the 2 pieces to be sewn right sides together and insert the alignment pin into the wrong side of the top piece at the point to be matched, and into the right side of the other point on the second piece, exiting through to the wrong side. Pull the pin down straight and snug so the pin end or head rests on the fabric and is exactly matching the 2 points. If the pin shaft is tilted even slightly, you are skewing and shifting the points and they will not be matched.

2. To secure the area for sewing, simultaneously hold the 2 pieces to be matched and the alignment pin straight with one hand and insert another pin just to the left (1⁄16″) of the alignment pin. Place another pin just to the right (1 1⁄16″) of the alignment pin. Then remove the alignment pin. If after sewing the points are not matched, you have pinned, sewed, or identified the area to be matched improperly and you need to correct it.

Noteworthy

In my experience, I have discovered that when you insert the alignment pin into the point from the wrong side of the fabric, it often exits out the right side incorrectly. To remedy this, when you insert the pin from the wrong side, look at how the pin exits out the right side to be sure it is at the exact point.

Matching Open Diamond Seams

This type of intersection occurs in the Lone Star block in *Lotus Flower* (page 112) and *Fire Fly* (page 67) when joining and matching 45° diamond intersections. This is the one time I always use an alignment pin.

1. Place the 2 cut segments right sides together and identify the correct edge to be sewn. Measure down from that edge ¼″ and make a mark on the seam. You can also use a template to make the ¼″ mark (see Accurate Templates, page 33).

2. Turn the pair of segments over and make a mark on that seam ¼″ down from the same edge. This creates a place to align and pin the intersection correctly.

3. To match this intersection, pin through the mark and seam of 1 piece and into the seam and mark of the other piece. Whether the seams are open or opposing, the pin must travel through the thread area and not into any fabric.

4. Pull the pin down, keeping the edges even. Secure the area by placing a pin just to the left and right of the alignment pin, and then remove the alignment pin. If the intersection is not matched, you either identified, pinned, or sewed improperly and you need to correct it. You must sew over the marks you make.

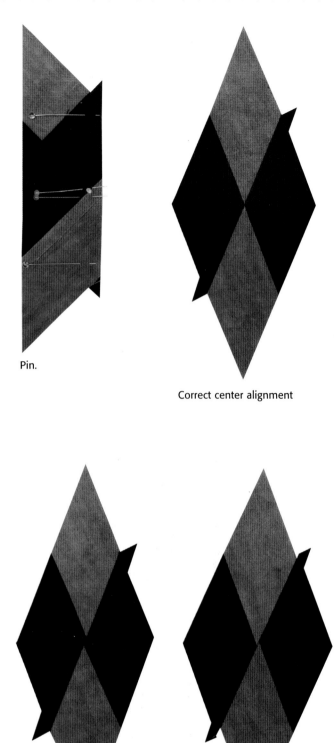

Pin.

Correct center alignment

Pin through marks.

Alignment pin

Seam allowance too wide

Seam allowance too narrow

Very Narrow (¹⁄₈″) Borders

Very narrow (⅛″) borders can give unexpected sparkle and detail to quilts, garments, or blocks and create an opportunity to use very hot, dark, or intense color proportionately and effectively. This technique can be used for borders (sewn together with other fabric borders and mitered or added separately in a boxed-corner fashion) or in strip units to be used with a template. When strip units are created and used with a template, this technique can also be used to interrupt side triangles and corners in a diagonal set, or to fracture shapes within patchwork blocks. The opportunities for application are endless.

I originally developed this technique to add proportional border widths to very small or intricate work. I wanted the narrow strip to be sewn in like a border, rather than a folded piece of fabric (flange) sewn between borders. Over time, the folded strip can begin to look untidy because the fold of the flange is loose and not sewn down, and it can get wrinkled when the quilt is folded and unfolded.

You can add these very narrow ⅛″ borders to your quilt separately, as you would a boxed corner, or you can join multiple border strips, including the ⅛″ border, then add them to your quilt as one border and miter the corners.

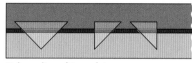

Strip unit and templates

Design within side and corner triangles

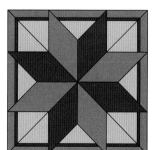

Fracture shapes within blocks

Conceptually, the technique used to create these borders is twofold. First, oversize by ⅜″ the width of the border you want to finish to ⅛″ and the border that follows it, for stability while sewing; and second, trim the appropriate ¼″ seam allowance to an exact ⅛″. This cut edge then serves as the sewing guide when adding the next border. The success of this technique depends on the accurate trimming of the ¼″ seam allowance to an exact ⅛″ and on sewing very straight, right along the cut edge of the just-trimmed seam allowance.

To determine how wide to cut your border strips you must first know how wide the finished width will be. For example, imagine you want 3 borders. You want border 1 to finish to 1″, so you would cut a 1½″-wide strip. You want border 2 to finish to ⅛″, so you would cut a 1″-wide strip (⅛″ plus ½″ usual seam allowance plus ⅜″ extra = 1″). You want border 3 to finish to 2″, so you would cut 2⅞″-wide strips because it follows the ⅛″ border (2″ plus ½″ usual seam allowance plus ⅜″ extra = 2⅞″).

Noteworthy

The ⅜″ added width is adequate for stable sewing. However, this is not a magic number. It could just as well be ½″ or more—it just needs to be the same on all appropriate strips.

1. Using the above example of the 3 borders, sew border 1 to 2, right sides together, with an accurate ¼″ seam allowance. Trim this seam to an exact ⅛″ with a rotary cutter and ruler. Press the stitches and then press the seam allowance toward border 2.

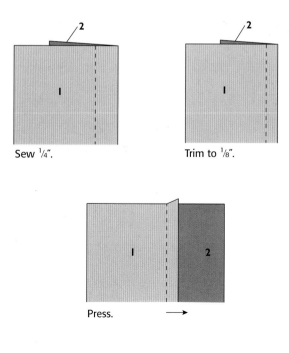

Sew ¼″.   Trim to ⅛″.

Press.

2. Place borders 3 and 1–2 right sides together, with border 1–2 on top and the edges aligned. Sew right along the just-trimmed seam allowance edge. This creates the ⅛″ border.

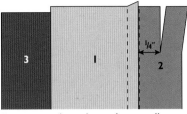

Sew next to just-trimmed seam allowance; trim excess to ¼″ from last stitches.

3. If the stitching meets your standards, trim the excess seam allowance to within ⅛″–¼″ from the last line of stitching, press the stitches, and press the seam toward border 3.

Finished ⅛″ border strip

Appliqué

Two projects in this book use both hand and machine appliqué, *Petite Sirah* (page 88) and *Fleur-de-Lis* (page 76). Preparation of the shapes, however, is exactly the same. This is a technique developed by Pearl P. Pereira of San Marcos, California, which I find invaluable. It has enabled me to appliqué successfully with no stress and has given me a great deal of confidence in continuing to add appliqué to my pieced quilts in the future. Please refer to Sources (page 124) for information about Pearl's available patterns and video.

Shape Preparation

This is a freezer-paper method of appliqué.

1. Layer 2 sheets of freezer paper, shiny side to dull side, and press them together smoothly so there are no wrinkles. Using 2 layers creates a crisper, more rigid edge to bring the fabric over and allows the shapes to be used many times. Pressing the 2 layers of freezer paper together also preshrinks the paper, so the shapes will not become distorted.

2. Trace the appliqué shapes onto the dull side of the layered freezer paper and cut them out exactly. The pieces that need to be reversed will be noted; all other shapes are symmetrical.

3. Press each paper shape, shiny side down, onto the wrong side of the appropriate fabric. If the fabric print does not dictate placement, place the shapes on the bias, leaving adequate room between them for the seam allowance. Cut around each freezer-paper shape, allowing a ³⁄₁₆″–¼″ seam allowance.

4. Spray starch in a small glass bowl. Dip a small stencil brush into the starch and wet the fabric seam allowance with the starch.

5. Using a stiletto or similar tool (I use a toothpick), bring the wet starched fabric over the paper edge, a little at a time, while using the iron to press and dry the fabric in place.

6. When all the seam allowance has been pressed over the paper edge, turn the shape right side up and press. This warms the freezer paper enough that you can now easily remove it by turning the piece back over, lifting a section of the seam allowance, and removing the paper shape. Re-press the fabric shape and store it in a baggie. The seam allowance will stay pressed in place, ready to be appliquéd by either hand or machine.

The advantages of this technique are that you have no paper to remove after you appliqué, so you do not need to cut the back of your work, you will not appliqué through the paper edge, the shapes are exact, the starch is easily removed by washing when your quilt is complete, and you can prepare all the shapes in advance before appliquéing.

7. Prepare the background as discussed in each project's instructions.

8. Glue baste the shapes in place for appliqué, using a very tiny amount of Roxanne's water-soluble Glue-Baste-It, being careful to keep the glue away from the edge you will be appliquéing.

9. I hand appliqué with #100 silk thread in a matching or camouflaging color and a Roxanne's #11 Betweens needle.

10. Press the finished appliqué from the back on a soft surface.

The Projects

*Focus on how well, not how fast,
you create your quilts.*

Shadowbox Baskets

French Confection

Fire Fly

Fleur-de-Lis

The projects are presented in order of difficulty. Once you have chosen a project, I suggest that you read the instructions completely to become familiar with the techniques that are used and the sequence of assembly. I encourage you to use these projects to your own best advantage. Feel free to duplicate them exactly or use different techniques; change the sets, their colors, or the size; or move one design element from one project to another. Add your own fresh ideas to create new designs that reflect your creative spirit. My hope is that you will reach for your personal best while enjoying the process. The relevance to the projects of all specific information presented in the process section (pages 9–54) and its importance in achieving quality workmanship is implied and is not repeated in the project instructions. Arrows indicate pressing direction; circles indicate an open seam.

Petite Sirah

Pieceful

Lotus Flower

Shadowbox Baskets

4¾" × 4¾" unfinished

Designed, machine pieced, and hand and machine quilted by author

Color

Rather than using an inspiration object or palette fabric from which to choose my colors, I chose to work in pinks and browns with an accent of green because I wanted an old-fashioned look and feel. Each of the basket backgrounds and small half-square triangles is a different fabric. The larger half-square triangle is the same fabric for all four baskets and is a multicolored print that incorporates the three colors I chose. In such a small quilt, exaggerated contrast and simplicity of design work best.

Design

Basket blocks are simple to sew and work beautifully on point, so they were a perfect candidate for this quilt. Based on the size of the back wall of the box, I knew I only had about 4½″ of space, so I placed four 1″ baskets on point, bordered them, and added pieced corner triangles to add some detail. A final border completes the quilt.

Vital Statistics:

- Block Size: 1″ finished, 1½″ unfinished
- Drafting Category: Four-patch, 4×4 grid
- Grid Dimension: ¼″
- Number of Shapes: 4
- Number of Pieces: 19

Techniques Used: templates (page 31), rotary cutting (page 30), creating straight strip units (page 47), stitched grid (page 41), square-to-square (page 42), very narrow (⅛″) borders (page 53), trimming seams (page 39), oversizing and custom cutting (page 40), and matching seams in same direction (page 49)

Fabric Requirements

- Basket Blocks: 6″ × 6″ squares of a variety of pinks and browns
- Accent Fabric: Quilter's fat quarter
- Corner Triangles and Border: Quilter's fat quarters of a variety of fabrics

Center Design

Basket Blocks

Instructions to make 1 Basket block:

The seven A/A units will be created using the stitched-grid technique (page 41), and the one B/B unit will be created using the square-to-square technique (page 42). Both will be oversized and custom cut (page 40).

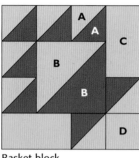

Basket block

Shape A: Cut 1 square 3″ × 3″ each from the basket and background fabric. On the lightest one, draw lines diagonally, horizontally, and vertically.

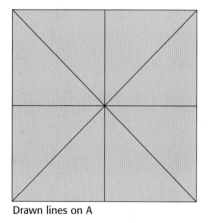

Drawn lines on A

Shape B: Cut 1 square 1½″ × 1½″ each from the basket and background fabric. Draw a diagonal line from corner to corner.

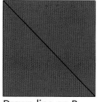

Drawn line on B

Shape C: Cut 2 rectangles 1″ × ¾″ from the background fabric.

Shape D: Cut 1 square ¾″ × ¾″ from the background fabric.

1. For the A/A units refer to Stitched-Grid Technique (page 41). You only need 7 units; the eighth unit is extra. Custom cut a ¾″ × ¾″ square from each oversized A/A unit (page 40).

2. For the B/B unit, refer to Square-to-Square Technique (page 42). Custom cut a 1″ × 1″ square.

3. Lay out all the basket pieces and assemble the basket. It should measure 1½″ × 1½″ square, unfinished. Make 3 more baskets.

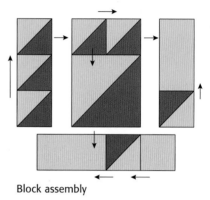

Block assembly

4. Join 2 baskets. Press the seam open and trim. Repeat for the other 2 baskets. Join the pairs to create the center quilt design, which measures 2½″ × 2½″ unfinished. Press the seam open and trim.

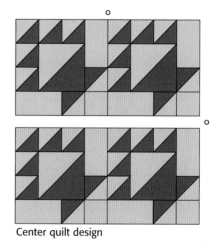

Center quilt design

Accent Border

1. Cut 2 strips of accent fabric ⅝″ × 2½″; add to 2 opposite sides.

2. Cut 2 strips of accent fabric ⅝″ × 2¾″; add to the other 2 sides. With the addition of the accent border, the design now measures 2¾″ × 2¾″ unfinished.

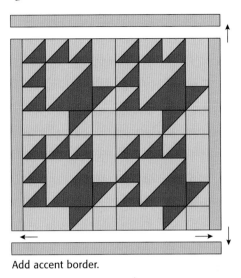

Add accent border.

Corner Triangles

The corner triangles are created by cutting shape E from a strip unit. Refer to Creating Straight Strip Units (page 47) and Very Narrow (⅛″) Borders (page 53). Make a template for shape E, transferring all the lines from the pattern to the template.

- Strip 1: Cut 1 strip 1″ × 20″.
- Strip 2: Cut 1 strip 1″ × 20″ (eventual ⅛″ strip).
- Strip 3: Cut 1 strip 1½″ × 20″.

1. Sew strip 1 to strip 2. Trim the ¼″ seam to an exact ⅛″ and press it toward strip 2.

2. Sew strip 1/2 to strip 3. Align the raw edges but sew next to the just-trimmed seam allowance. Press toward strip 3 and trim the excess to ⅛″ from the last line of stitching.

3. Cut 8 shape Es from the strip unit; align the lines on the template with the seamlines.

4. Join 2 shape Es. Make 4. Refer to matching seams in same direction (page 49).

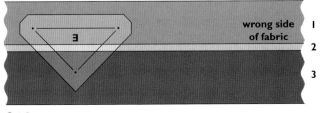

wrong side of fabric
I
2
3

Cut 8.

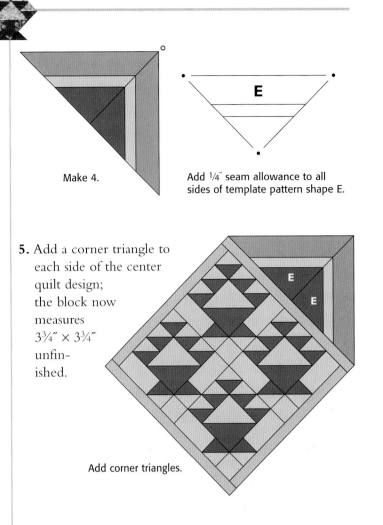

Make 4.

E

Add ¼″ seam allowance to all sides of template pattern shape E.

5. Add a corner triangle to each side of the center quilt design; the block now measures 3¾″ × 3¾″ unfinished.

E
E

Add corner triangles.

Final Border

1. Cut 2 strips 1″ × 3¾″ and add to the sides.

2. Cut 2 strips 1″ × 4¾″ and add to the top and bottom.

3. The quilt top is now complete. After quilting, trim the final border ⅝″ from the last seam and bind with ⅛″ finished binding.

Add the final border.

Shadowbox Baskets   59

French Confection

14¾″ × 17½″ unfinished

Designed, machine pieced, and hand and machine quilted by author

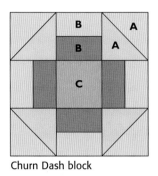

Color

This quilt is simple to sew, so the fun and challenge lie in using many different fabrics. My color inspiration (red, turquoise, and yellow) came from a bedding ad in a catalog. I was able to find a fabric that embraced the same colors, French feeling, and character as that ad. My impression of the French style combines a variety of busy, pretty, floral prints, which replaces the high-value contrast I usually use with a subtler, lower-value contrast. Once I found the palette fabric, I chose a variety of values and visual textures for each color, expanding their potential to create a full palette. In the end, I used 46 different fabrics. I placed the smaller, tightly spaced prints in the smaller shapes, the medium-scaled prints in the centers of the blocks, and the larger-scaled prints in the alternate blocks, side triangles, and corners. The series of four borders repeats the colors, and the final border print in a darker tone-on-tone turquoise brings the design to a lovely conclusion. Refer to Color and Fabric (pages 11–17) to see how I developed the fabric and color choices for this quilt.

Design

This very traditional, uncomplicated design consists of twelve 1½″ Churn Dash blocks that are sashed, set on point, and then surrounded by alternate blocks, side triangles, and corners. Four narrow borders (¼″, ⅝″, ⅛″, and ⅜″) are followed by a wider 1½″ border print.

Vital Statistics:

- Block Size: 1½″ finished, 2″ unfinished
- Drafting Category: Nine-patch, 3×3 grid
- Grid Dimension: ½″
- Number of Shapes: 3
- Number of Pieces: 17

Techniques Used: individual half-square triangles (page 40), creating straight strip units (page 47), oversizing and custom cutting (page 40), very narrow (⅛″) borders (page 53), rotary cutting (page 30), templates (page 31), and trimming seams (page 39).

Fabric Requirements

- Block Fabrics: Fat eighths of a variety of colors and visual textures
- Sashing: ⅛ yard

- Alternate Blocks, Side Triangles, and Corners: ¼ yard
- Borders: To cut on the length grain you will need a quilter's fat quarter for each of the 4 narrow borders and ⅔ yard for the final border.

Churn Dash Blocks

Instructions to make 1 Churn Dash block:

Churn Dash block

Shapes A and B are cut oversized and custom cut (page 40).

- Shape A: Cut 2 squares 1¾″ × 1¾″ each of background and block fabrics; cut in half diagonally.
- Shape B: Cut 1 strip 1″ × 7″ each of background and block fabrics.
- Shape C: Cut 1 square 1″ × 1″ for the center; make it interesting.

1. Stitch a background and a block fabric A triangle together. Make 4.

2. Custom cut a 1″ × 1″ square from each unit.

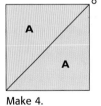

Make 4.

Custom cut a 1″ × 1″ square.

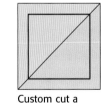

Cut 4 squares 1″ × 1″.

3. Sew the background and block fabric B strips together. Press the seam open and trim.

4. On 1 end, make a straight cleanup cut by placing a horizontal line of the ruler on the seam and cutting the excess.

5. Rotate the strip unit and cut 4 segments 1″ wide.

6. Custom cut each 1″ segment into a 1″ × 1″ square by cutting ½″ from the center seam in both directions.

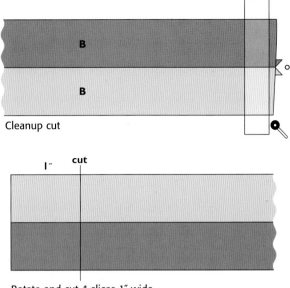

Cleanup cut

1″   cut

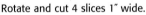

Rotate and cut 4 slices 1″ wide.

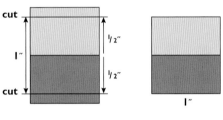

Custom cut 4 squares 1″ × 1″.

7. Lay out the block. Assemble the units into rows and the rows into the complete block, which measures 2″ × 2″ unfinished. Make 12.

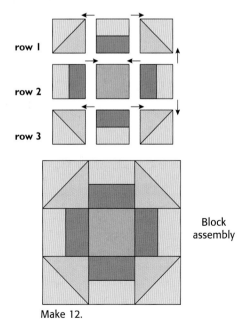

row 1

row 2

row 3

Block assembly

Make 12.

Sashing

- Cut 3 strips ¾″ × 40″ from the sashing fabric; subcut 24 rectangles ¾″ × 2″ and 24 rectangles ¾″ × 2½″.

Noteworthy

As you add the sashing to the blocks, it is important to sew straight and maintain the complete, sharp points on the triangles.

1. Sew a ¾″ × 2″ sashing strip to opposite sides of each block.

2. Sew a ¾″ × 2½″ sashing strip to the remaining 2 sides of each block, which now measures 2½″ × 2½″ unfinished.

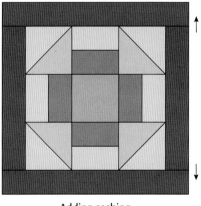

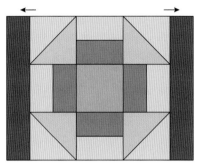

Adding sashing

Alternate Blocks, Side Triangles, and Corners

Make templates for shapes D and E (page 63).
- Shape D: Cut 10 from side triangle fabric.
- Shape E: Cut 4 from corner fabric.
- Cut 6 squares 2½″ × 2½″ from alternate block fabric.

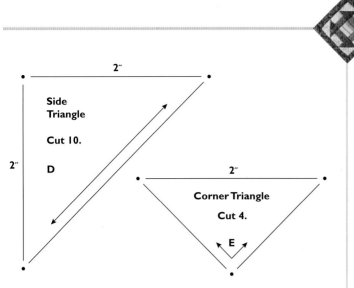

Add ¼″ seam allowance to all sides of each shape.

1. Lay out the 12 sashed blocks with the 6 alternate blocks, 10 side triangles, and 4 corners.

2. Assemble in diagonal rows and press toward the alternate blocks, side triangles, and corners.

3. Now join the rows, matching and pinning the intersections. For the quilt top to lie flat and square, the seam allowances must lie toward the alternate blocks, side triangles, and corners. To make this happen, you will need to clip into the seam allowance (not the stitching) at the intersections to release the seam allowance and enable it to redirect itself.

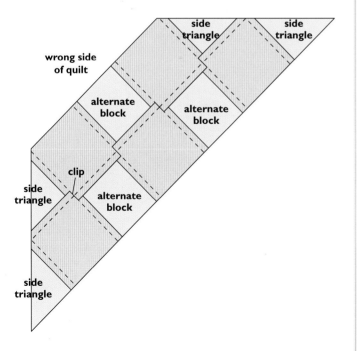

Clip into the seam allowance to redirect it.

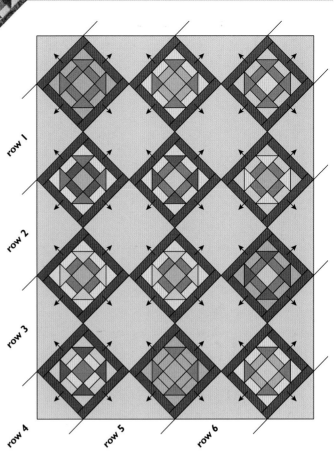

Quilt top assembly and pressing paths

Borders

Familiarize yourself with Creating Straight Strip Units (page 47) and Very Narrow (⅛″) Borders (page 53) before adding borders 3 and 4, since this information applies to them.

Five borders are added to this quilt. Four are added in a boxed-corner fashion, and the fifth and final border is mitered because I used a border print. If you do not use a fabric that requires mitering or do not choose to miter, your fifth border can be added in a boxed-corner fashion as well. The instructions explain how to do both.

Border 1 finishes ¼″ wide (cut ¾″ wide).
Border 2 finishes ⅝″ wide (cut 1⅛″ wide).
Border 3 finishes ⅛″ wide (cut 1″ wide).
Border 4 finishes ⅜″ wide (cut 1¼″ wide).
Border 5 finishes 1½″ wide (cut 2″ wide).

Boxed Corners

1. Measure your quilt vertically through the center. Cut 2 strips of your chosen fabric that exact length and ¾″ wide.

2. Fold the 2 strips in half and crease them to identify the center. At the ironing board align, press, and pin the edges of the border and quilt right sides together, matching and pinning the centers and ends of both together. Add additional pins parallel to the edge.

3. Sew with a ¼" seam allowance, removing the pins as you approach them.

4. Press the stitches, then press the seam allowance toward the border.

5. Measure your quilt horizontally across the center and cut 2 strips of the same fabric that exact length and ¾" wide. Add to the top and bottom of the quilt.

6. Add borders 2, 3, and 4 in the same manner as border 1. Check to be sure your corners are 90° before adding each consecutive border.

Adding boxed-corner borders

Final Border, Symmetrical Border Print Option

To create mirror-image corners and have the fabric design appear to travel around the quilt in an uninterrupted fashion you must have a symmetrical border print design. Be sure your border print design is also proportional relative to the size of the quilt. To audition two corner choices, first identify a whole motif and the area between motifs.

1. Measure your quilt horizontally from edge to edge and deduct ½". This is the finished quilt width.

2. Measure from the center of a whole motif one-half the finished quilt width and place a mirror at a 45° angle from that miter point toward the outer edge of the border to view the corner design. Do the same from the area between 2 motifs and choose 1 corner design.

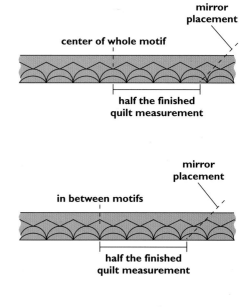

Interview corner design

3. Based on the corner design you chose, cut 2 border strips for the top and bottom 2" wide by the finished quilt width plus twice the width of the border plus approximately 3" for mitering excess.

4. On the wrong side of both the top and bottom border strips, mark the area you will place at the center of the quilt. Then measure out one-half the finished width of the quilt from the center in both directions and make a mark ¼" from the edge. This is the miter point.

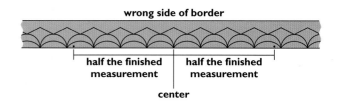

Marking miter point on top and bottom borders

5. Measure the quilt vertically and cut 2 more strips approximately 10˝ longer than the first 2 strips.

6. Lay the top border right side up on top of 1 side border (also right side up) toward 1 end, matching the fabric print exactly and allowing mitering overlap space. Place a dot on the side border in exactly the same place as it appears on the top border. Measure out from that dot half the finished length of the quilt plus ¼˝ and cut.

7. You now have one-half of 1 side border, which serves as the template for the other 3 half side borders.

8. Take this half side border and place it at the other end of the same side border you've been working on, right sides together, creating a mirror image and matching the fabric print exactly. Make a miter dot on the wrong side of the border exactly where it appears on the "template" border. Measure out one-half the finished length measurement of the quilt plus ¼˝ and cut.

9. Repeat this process for the remaining side border.

10. Sew the 2 halves together to create a side border. Make 2. Press the seams open. The seams on the side borders will hardly be noticeable because they create a mirror image.

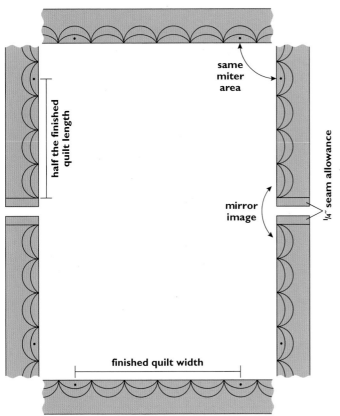

Creating side borders

Final Border, Plain-Fabric Option

1. Measure your quilt both vertically and horizontally, then subtract ½˝ from each and write those measurements down.

2. Cut 2 border strips for the top and bottom that equal the horizontal measurement plus twice the width of the border plus 3˝. Cut 2 border strips for the sides that equal the vertical measurement plus twice the width of the border plus 3˝.

3. On the wrong side of all 4 borders, mark the center, then measure out from the center one-half the finished measurement in both directions on the appropriate border strips and make a mark ¼˝ from the edge, as you did for the top and bottom borders if using a symmetrical border print.

ADDING THE BORDERS

To create a flat, smooth mitered corner you must stop sewing ¼˝ from the corner and backstitch when adding the borders to the quilt top.

1. On the wrong side of the quilt top, make dots ¼˝ from both edges at each corner and at the center of each side.

2. At the ironing board, place 1 border onto the quilt top, right sides together. Match and pin the center and ¼˝ marks on both, aligning their edges exactly. Place additional pins parallel to the edge.

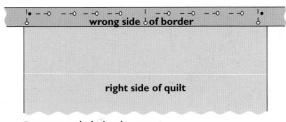

Recommended pin placement

3. Lower the needle just in front of the dot, and with a small stitch length take 3 stitches forward and back. Return to your usual stitch length and sew to ½˝ from the opposite miter point, then reduce the stitch length again, stop sewing just in front of the miter mark, and backstitch 3 stitches. Remove the piece from the machine. Repeat for the remaining 3 borders. Press toward the border.

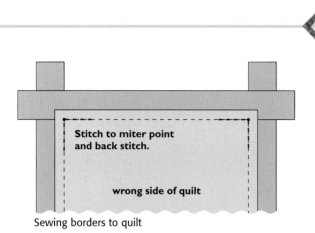

Stitch to miter point
and back stitch.

wrong side of quilt

Sewing borders to quilt

FORMING THE MITERED CORNERS BY HAND

Appliquéing the miter closed from the outside corner inward will keep the corner squarer. Which border is over the other when you are forming the miter depends on how you position yourself to appliqué.

1. At the ironing board, position 1 corner of your quilt right side up. Be sure the quilt is supported and not hanging off the surface, pulling and distorting the corner.

2. Fold 1 border at a 45° angle over the opposite border, aligning both edges.

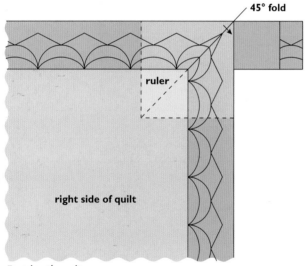

45° fold

ruler

right side of quilt

Forming the miter

3. Align each mitered fold with the 45° line on a large square ruler. The border edges must align with the outside edges of the ruler, which creates the necessary 90° corner. Press, pin, and baste the miter fold in place. Trim the excess to within ½″ of the fold. Repeat for the remaining 3 corners.

4. Hand appliqué the miter fold closed, working from the outside corner to the miter point. Use a matching thread and very small stitches. Trim the seam allowance to ¼″ and press the seam to one side, not open. The quilt top is complete.

Fire Fly

20¼″ × 20¼″ unfinished

Designed, machine pieced, and hand and machine quilted by author

Color

The paisley fabric in the tree trunk and border was used as the palette fabric for this project, although I adjusted the color proportions. A variety of values and visual textures of only three colors—red, gold, and navy blue, with an accent of turquoise—creates a balance of warm and cool colors.

Design

This project, which I had envisioned for a long time, was inspired by the beauty of nature: a lone, statuesque tree surrounded by stars and Flying Geese, embraced by a midnight-blue sky. The tree block is bordered and set on point, then corner triangles are added to incorporate half-stars. Another border is added, then more half-stars and corner detail. Subtle Flying Geese travel around the tree and stars, and finally a series of four borders is added to frame the piece.

Vital Statistics:

- Tree Size: 5″ finished, 5½″ unfinished
- Drafting Category: Five-patch, 10×10 grid
- Grid Dimension: ½″
- Number of Shapes: 7
- Number of Pieces: 99
- Half-Star Size: One-half of a 3″ block
- Drafting Category: Eight-pointed star
- Grid Dimension: N/A
- Number of Shapes: 3
- Number of Pieces: 21

Techniques Used: rotary cutting (page 30), double half-square triangles (page 45), individual half-square triangles (page 40), templates (page 31), very narrow (⅛″) borders (page 53), oversizing and custom cutting (page 40), mirrors/mock-ups (page 26), creating straight strip units (page 47), trimming seams (page 39), and matching seams in the same direction (page 49)

Fabric Requirements

- Background and Final Border: 1¼ yards total of dark blue
- Geese and Borders: ⅓ yard of bright blue
- Star Diamonds and Border: ¼ yard each of 2 reds (fabrics 1 and 2)
- Diamonds: ⅛ yard of yellow (fabric 3)
- Tree Leaves: ¼ yard total of a variety of colors
- Tree Trunk, Corners, and Border: ⅜ yard of paisley
- Border: ¼ yard of turquoise

Noteworthy

One approach to color and fabric placement for the tree is to mock up half the tree on a chosen background, then place a mirror along the edge to see the whole tree and create a color map (page 26).

Center Design

Tree Block

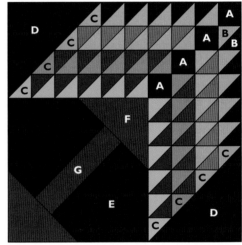

Tree block

Make a template for shape E.

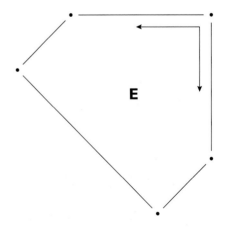

Add ¼″ seam allowance to all sides of shape E.

- Shape A: Cut 4 squares 1″ × 1″ from background fabric.

- Shape B: Cut 5 squares 1⅝″ × 1⅝″ from background fabric; cut in half diagonally (this will yield the 10 triangles that appear at the upper 2 edges of the tree block). Cut 35 squares 1⅝″ × 1⅝″ from an assortment of tree fabrics based on your mock-up; cut in half diagonally (this will yield 70 triangles, 35 for each half of the tree).

- Shape C: Cut 4 squares 1⅜″ × 1⅜″ from tree fabrics; cut in half diagonally (this will yield 8 triangles, 4 for each half of the tree).

- Shape D: Cut 1 square 2⅞″ × 2⅞″ from background fabric; cut in half diagonally.

- Shape E: Cut 2 from background fabric.

- Shape F: Cut 1 square 2⅜″ × 2⅜″ from trunk fabric; cut in half diagonally.

- Shape G: Cut 1 rectangle 1″ × 2⅝″ from trunk fabric.

1. Referring to your half-tree mock-up, pair 80 B triangles to create 40 half-square triangle units. Sew from point to point, press the seams open, trim the seams, and custom cut a 1″ × 1″ square from each. The C triangles are left single and added to their appropriate rows. Refer to Individual Half-Square Triangles (page 40) and Oversize and Custom-Cut Technique (page 40).

2. Lay out the tree block shapes and assemble into 3 units. Unit 1 should measure 2½″ × 3½″ unfinished, unit 2 should measure 2½″ × 5½″ unfinished, and the trunk unit should measure 3½″ × 3½″ unfinished.

3. Join unit 1 to the trunk unit. Add unit 2 to unit 1 / trunk unit. The block measures 5½″ × 5½″ unfinished.

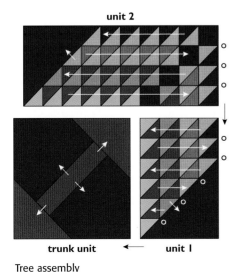

unit 2

trunk unit ← unit I

Tree assembly

¼″ Border

1. Cut 2 strips ¾″ × 5½″ from bright blue fabric and add to opposite sides of the tree block.

2. Cut 2 strips ¾″ × 6″ from bright blue fabric and add to the other 2 sides of the tree block, which now measures 6″ × 6″ unfinished.

Corner Triangles

Placing the block on point requires that a triangle be sewn onto each edge of the block to square the design. Each triangle incorporates a 3″ Half Morning Star block combined with background shapes.

Block with corner triangles

3″ Half Morning Star Blocks

Make templates for shapes H, I, J★, and K. When making shape J, extend the interior lines to the edge of the template.

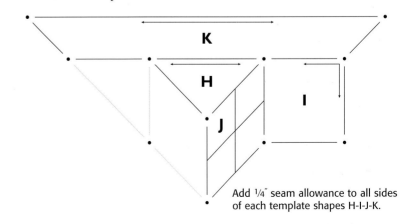

Add ¼″ seam allowance to all sides of each template shapes H-I-J-K.

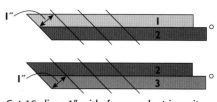

- Shape H: Cut 16 from background fabric.
- Shape I: Cut 4 from background fabric.
- ★Shape J: Cut 16 from strip units.
- Shape K: Cut 8 from background fabric.
- ★Each shape J diamond consists of 4 smaller diamonds. There are 3 positions of color within the J shape. The position 1 fabric/color congregates in the center and creates a smaller half-star. The position 2 fabric/color is used twice as much, so it is dominant, and position 3 creates the star points, which touch the background, so you must create high contrast to see them.

Noteworthy

To determine the best choice for the diamonds, audition different fabric and color choices by cutting 4 small diamonds (cut $1/2$″ × 2″ short strips of possible choices, cut a 45° angle at one end, then cut $1/2$″ slices to create the diamonds). This is not exact but will give you an approximate finished size to audition color. Arrange 4 small diamonds as illustrated on your background fabric and use mirrors (from both ends) to see a whole star. Mix, match, and change until you find the best choice. (Rough cut mock-up, page 26).

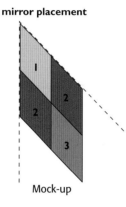

mirror placement

Mock-up

Strip Unit
- Cut 1 strip 1″ × 40″ each from fabrics 1 and 3 based on the mock-up.
- Cut 2 strips 1″ × 40″ from fabric 2.

1. Sew fabric strips 1 and 2 together lengthwise, offsetting by the width of the cut strips, then press the seam open and trim the seam. Sew fabric strips 2 and 3 together similarly. Refer to Creating Straight Strip Units (page 47).

2. With the fabric strips right side up, cut a 45° angle on the end of each strip unit and cut 16 slices 1″ wide from each strip unit. To maintain the correct angle, always keep the 45° angle line of the ruler on the seam and the 1″ line of the ruler on the edge of the fabric. When you cannot place these 2 lines appropriately, it simply means the angle has tipped off and you need to reestablish it again.

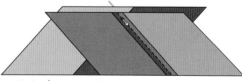

Cut 16 slices 1″ wide from each strip unit.

3. Create 1 diamond at a time. Lay out 1 slice from each strip unit appropriately. Pick up the 2 slices, right sides together, being aware of which edge will be sewn.

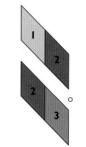

Create one diamond at a time.

4. Make a dot ¼″ down from the correct edge, over the seam (you can use template J to do this). Refer to Accurate Templates (page 33). Turn the paired slices over and make a second mark similarly.

5. Use the alignment-pin technique (page 51) to pin the intersections. Refer to Matching Open Diamond Seams (page 51).

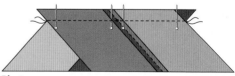

Mark dot ¼″ from edge on seam. Pin through both pieces to align seams.

Pin to secure seams.

Match center intersection.

6. Sew the 2 slices, sewing over the marks. You can also draw a line through the dot to create a sewing line, although you must still mark and match the intersection with the alignment pin. See page 52 if your intersection is not matched exactly.

7. When the intersection is matched, press the seam open and trim. Repeat Steps 3–7 for the remaining 15 diamonds.

8. These 16 diamonds are oversized and must now be custom cut to the appropriate size. Place the J template face up onto the right side of 1 oversized diamond. Align the template lines with the seamlines exactly. Cut around the template with the small 18mm rotary cutter (see Accurate Templates, page 31). Do not mark the dots onto the right side of the fabric. To mark the dots, remove the template and place it face down on the wrong side of the fabric diamond. Mark the dots with a tool that will not bleed through to the right side of the fabric but one you can see clearly. Repeat for the remaining 15 diamonds.

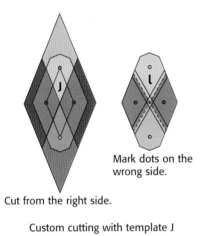

Mark dots on the
wrong side.

Cut from the right side.

Custom cutting with template J

Noteworthy

I cut and then mark the dots in two steps because I can see more clearly from the right side to match the template lines to the seamlines; then I turn the template and fabric diamond over to mark the dots.

Assembling Half Morning Stars

1. Lay out 1 Half Morning Star block. Refer to Y-Seam Construction (page 46). Y-seam areas are indicated by a +.

2. Set up your work to look like the illustration as you assemble. Sew 2 Js to 1 H. Beginning at the outer edge, sew to the dot and backstitch. To accomplish this and sew from the edge both times, H will be on top once and J will be on top once. Sew the diamonds together. Beginning at the center edge, sew to the dot and backstitch. Press and trim the seams. Repeat.

3. Add an I square on the right side of 1 H/J/J unit. Beginning at the outside edge, sew to the dot and backstitch.

4. Add an H triangle on the right side of 1 H/J/J unit. Beginning at the outside edge, sew from edge to edge.

5. Join the H/J/J/I unit to the H/H/J/J unit by sewing I to J from the outside edge to the dot and then backstitching. Then join the J diamond edges. Stitch from the center edge to the dot and backstitch.

6. Now add the final H triangle, sewing from edge to edge. There will be 2 bias edges exposed temporarily; do not press or overhandle these.

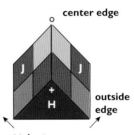

center edge

J J

+ H

outside edge

Make 2.

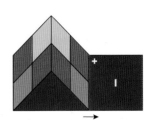

+

I

Make 1.

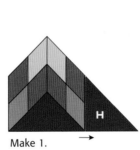

H

Make 1.

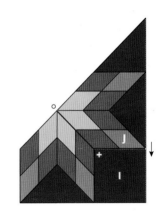

J

+

I

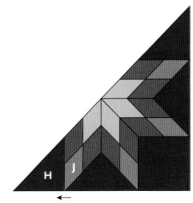

H J

Assembly sequence

7. Add 2 Ks to 1 Half Morning Star block, sewing from edge to dot and backstitching. Sew the corner miter seam from the outer edge to the dot and backstitch. Make 4.

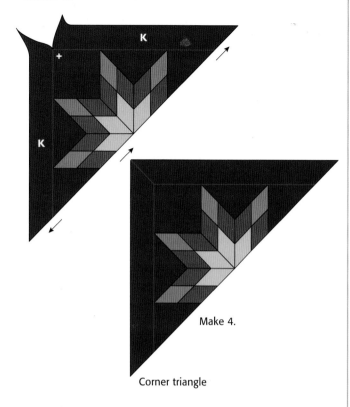

Make 4.

Corner triangle

8. On the wrong side of the bordered tree block, make a dot ¼″ from both edges at each corner(page 75).

9. Add an H/I/J/K corner triangle unit to each edge of the bordered tree block, matching and pinning at the dots and sewing from edge to edge. The quilt now measures 8¼″ × 8¼″ unfinished (page 75).

¼″ Border

1. Cut 2 strips ¾″ × 8¼″ from bright blue fabric, add to opposite sides of the quilt, and press toward the border.

2. Cut 2 strips ¾″ × 8¾″ from bright blue fabric, add to the top and bottom of the quilt, and press toward the border.

Design Border

Make a template for shape L (page 31), transferring all lines. Shape H and J templates are already made.

- Shape H: Cut 20 from background fabric.
- Shape J: Cut 16 from strip unit.
- Shape L: Cut 8 from strip unit.

Shape J Strip Unit

- Cut 1 strip 1″ × 40″ each from fabrics 1 and 3, referring to the mock-up.
- Cut 2 strips 1″ × 40″ from fabric 2, referring to the mock-up.
- Create 4 Half Morning Star blocks, referring to 3″ Half Morning Star Blocks (page 69) and replacing shape I (square) with H (triangle).

Shape L Strip Unit

- Cut 2 strips 1⅜″ × 40″ from background fabric.
- Cut 2 strips 1⅝″ × 40″ from paisley fabric.

1. Sew a background and a paisley fabric strip together and press the seam open. Make 2.

2. Place the shape L template face down on the wrong side of the strip unit, matching the seamline to the line on the template and paying attention to the fabric placement within the template shape. Cut 8.

3. Sew a shape L to each side of a Half Morning Star block, matching the dots and sewing from edge to edge.

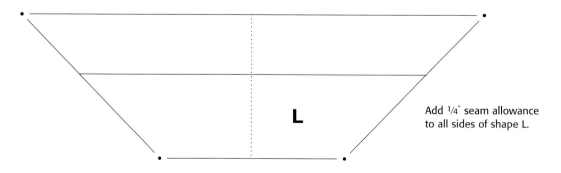

L

Add ¼″ seam allowance to all sides of shape L.

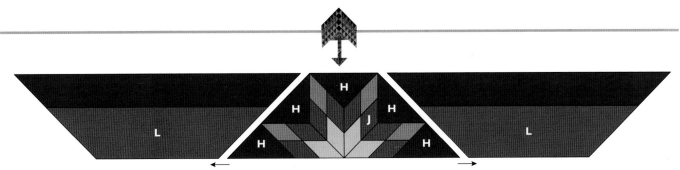

Design border assembly; make 4.

4. On the wrong side of the bordered quilt top, make a dot ¼″ from both edges at each corner. Add an L/Half Morning Star/L design border to each side of the quilt, matching dots, sewing from dot to dot, and backstitching (page 66).

5. Sew 4 corner miter seams from the outside edge to the dot, and backstitch. The quilt top now measures 11¾″ × 11¾″ unfinished.

Flying Geese Border

Refer to Double Half-Square Triangles (page 45) for assembly and pressing instructions.

⅜″ grid dimension (repeat unit length)

- Cut 128 rectangles ⅞″ × 1¼″ from bright blue for geese.
- Cut 256 squares ⅞″ × ⅞″ from background fabric.

Noteworthy

The Flying Geese unit must remain the exact size of the rectangle you start with.

1. Sew 30 Flying Geese units together and press toward the bright blue point. Make 4.

2. Referring to the illustration for the direction of the geese, add a 30-unit border to each side of the quilt and press toward the quilt.

3. Sew 2 Flying Geese units together for the corners. Make 4. Add a corner unit to each end of the remaining two 30-unit borders. Add to the top and bottom of the quilt. Press toward the quilt. The quilt top now measures 13¼″ × 13¼″ unfinished.

Whole-Fabric Borders

These 3 borders repeat the red/orange, turquoise, and paisley fabrics. They finish to ¼″, ⅛″, and ⅝″, respectively, and are added to the quilt top in a boxed-corner fashion, meaning that you add the 2 side borders, press, and then add the top and bottom borders.

Noteworthy

It is important that you have a clear understanding of the narrow-border technique (page 53), as it is used for borders 2 and 3.

Border 1 (red/orange)

- Cut 2 strips ¾″ × 13¼″ for the sides.
- Cut 2 strips ¾″ × 13¾″ for the top and bottom.

Border 1 finishes ¼″. Add the 2 side borders and press toward the border, then add the top and bottom borders and press toward the border.

Border 2 (turquoise)

- Cut 2 strips 1″ × 13¾″ for the sides.
- Cut 2 strips 1″ × 14¾″ for the top and bottom.

Border 2 finishes ⅛″. Add the 2 side borders, trim the ¼″ seam allowance to an exact ⅛″, and press toward the border. Add the top and bottom borders, trim the ¼″ seam allowance to an exact ⅛″, and press toward the border.

Border 3 (paisley)

- Cut 2 strips 1½″ × 14¾″ for the sides.
- Cut 2 strips 1½″ × 15¼″ for the top and bottom.

Border 3 finishes to ⅝″. Add the 2 side borders by aligning their edges with the border 2 edges, with border 3 on the bottom, and sewing carefully next to the trimmed seam allowance. Press the stitches, evaluate the ⅛″ border for straightness, and trim the excess seam allowance to ¼″

Add borders 1, 2, and 3.

from the last line of stitching. Add the top and bottom borders similarly. The quilt now measures 15¼″ × 15¼″ unfinished.

Final Whole-Fabric Border

This border is added to the quilt using the partial-seam corner technique. Refer to Creating Straight Strip Units (page 47) for instructions on how to align, press, and pin borders.

• Cut 4 length-grain strips 17¾″ × 3″ from dark blue.

1. Take 1 border and align it edge to edge with the right side of the quilt. Sew down about 3″ and remove the piece from the machine. Press the seam allowance toward the border.

2. Working in a counterclockwise direction, sew the remaining 3 borders to the quilt top, always pressing the seam allowances toward the border.

3. Sew the partial seam closed and press toward the border. The quilt now measures 20¼″ × 20¼″ unfinished.

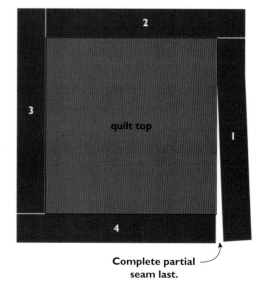

Add final border.

Fleur-de-Lis

51⅝″ × 51⅝″ unfinished

Designed, machine pieced, and appliquéd by author, machine
quilted by Jill Schumacher, Rio Vista, CA

Color

The color choices for *Fleur-de-Lis* are analogous (neighbors on the color wheel): purples, pinks, magentas, and a touch of blue (used only in the center square of the center pieced block and again for the ⅛″ narrow border). The majority of the background area is a peachy-pink/greenish mottled floral fabric that has subtle coloring, which complements the design colors and provides high contrast. A second light green fabric in the border area and a third light tan/purple/yellow fabric in the center offer a little variety without changing the character of the primary background color.

Design

This quilt combines piecing and appliqué in a contemporary medallion style. I wanted the center appliqué design and curved border element to play a starring role, and the Goose in the Pond blocks and pieced borders to be supportive. Although initially there was no relationship between the pieced blocks and the appliqué design, the addition of the checkerboard and sawtooth pieced border and the curved border design connected the two separate elements into a cohesive, successful design. The series of five plain fabric borders, all in different widths, quietly frames the simple design.

Vital Statistics:

- Block Size: 5⅝″ × 5⅝″ finished, 6⅛″ × 6⅛″ unfinished
- Grid Dimension: 1⅛″ (nine-patch grid dimension: ⅜″)
- Drafting Category: Five-patch, 5×5 grid
- Number of Shapes: 3
- Number of Pieces: 77

Techniques Used: individual half-square triangles (page 40), creating straight strip units (page 47), oversizing and custom cutting (page 40), appliqué (page 54), and rotary cutting (page 30)

Fabric Requirements

- Pieced Blocks, Curved Border Shape D, Checkerboard, and Final Plain Borders 2 and 4: Primary background, 2⅛ yards; secondary (greenish) background, 1⅝ yards; third background, ⅜ yard
- Appliqué Shapes J, K, and O; Pieced Blocks; Checkerboard; and Final Plain Border 3 (cross grain): 1¼ yards total of dark purples
- Appliqué Shapes L and P: ¾ yard of medium purple
- Appliqué Shapes G, H, and M; Curved Border Shape F; Final Plain Border 5 (length grain): 2 yards total of dark magentas
- Appliqué Shape I, Pieced Blocks, Sawtooth Border: 1⅛ yards total of medium magentas
- Appliqué Shape N, Curved Border Shape E, Center Square in Center Block: ¾ yard of pink
- Nine-Patch Centers in Center Block and Final Plain Border 1: ¼ yard of blue accent

Pieced Block

You will need a total of 5 blocks; the 4 corner blocks are all the same. The center block's nine-patches and center square are different in their color and value only. An asterisk (★) will indicate the center block differences. Refer to the photo of the quilt if necessary.

Instructions to make 1 Goose in the Pond block:

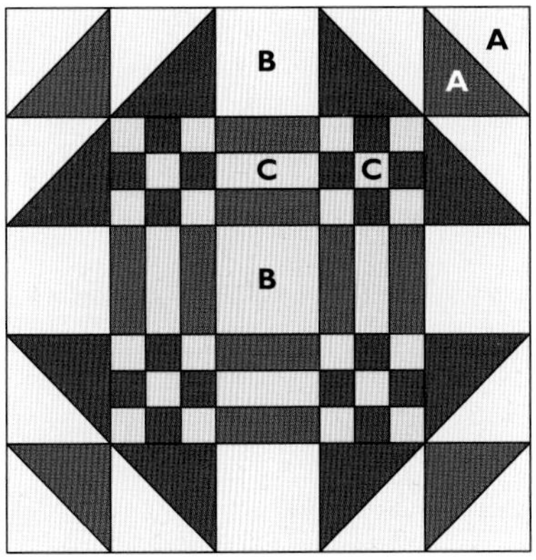

Goose in the Pond block

Shape A will be created using the individual half-square triangle technique (page 40) and the oversizing and custom-cutting technique (page 40). Shape C (nine-patches and rails) will be created and cut from strip units (page 47).

- Shape A: Cut 6 squares 2¼″ × 2¼″ of primary background and block fabric (4 from dark purple and 2 from medium magenta); cut in half diagonally.
- Shape B: Cut 5 squares 1⅝″ × 1⅝″ (4 of primary background and 1 of third background for center; ★4 of third background and ★1 of pink for center).
- Shape C nine-patches: Cut 3 strips ⅞″ × 8″ of both third background (light) and dark purple. ★Cut 2 strips ⅞″ × 8″ of third background. ★Cut 1 strip ⅞″ × 8″ of blue accent. ★Cut 3 strips ⅞″ × 8″ of medium magenta.

- Shape C rails: Cut 1 strip ⅞″ × 8″ of third background. Cut 2 strips ⅞″ × 8″ of medium magenta.

Shape A Construction

1⅛″ grid dimension

1. Sew a light triangle to each of 4 medium and 8 dark A triangles. Press the seams toward the darker triangles.
2. Custom cut a square 1⅝″ × 1⅝″ from each.

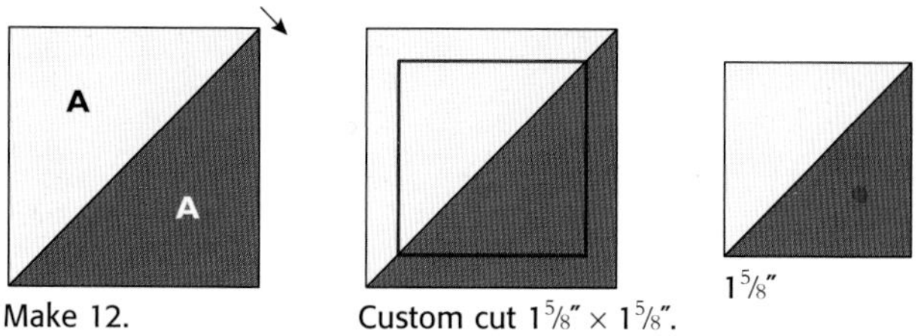
A
A
1⅝″
Make 12. Custom cut 1⅝″ × 1⅝″.

Shape C Nine-Patch Construction

⅜″ grid dimension

1. Sew 1 strip unit of dark/light/dark (★medium/blue/medium) and 1 strip unit of light/dark/light (★light/medium/light). Press after adding each strip and measure. Two strips sewn together should measure 1¼″ from edge to edge and 3 strips sewn should measure 1⅝″ from edge to edge. Press the seams in one direction and trim.

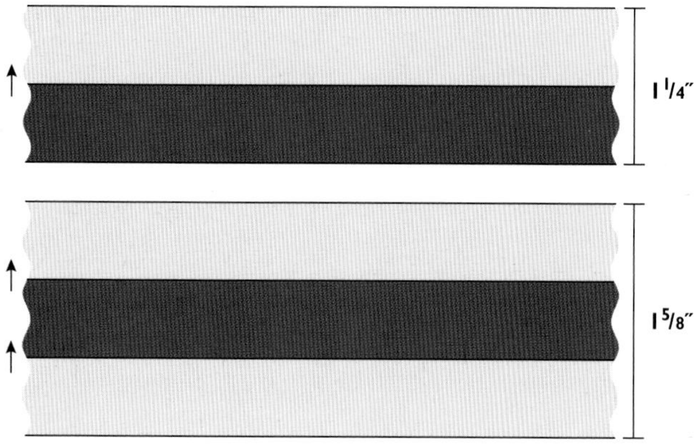
1¼″
1⅝″
Strip units

2. From the light/dark/light (★light/medium/light) strip unit, cut 8 segments ⅞″ wide.
3. From the dark/light/dark (★medium/blue/medium) strip unit, cut 4 segments ⅞″ wide.

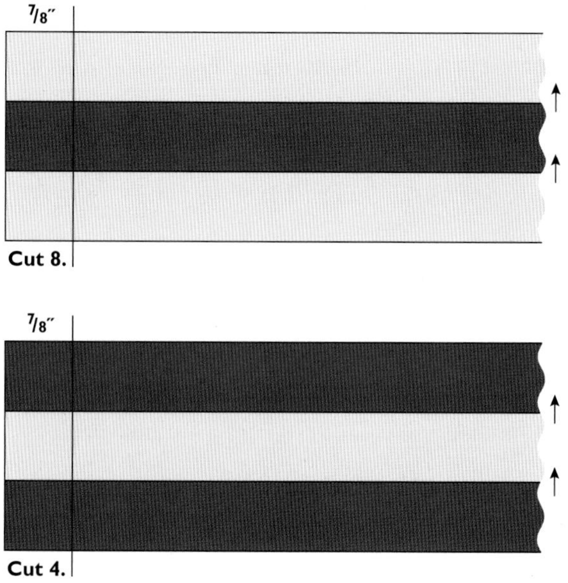
⅞″
Cut 8.
⅞″
Cut 4.
Cutting segments

4. Pair 1 light/dark/light segment (★light/medium/light) to a dark/light/dark (★medium/blue/medium) segment. Make 4. Arrange the segments to create opposing seams and chain piece the 4 pairs, keeping the bottom seam allowance smooth as they go over the feed dogs if necessary. Two segments sewn should measure 1¼″ × 1⅝″. Trim the seams.
5. Repeat to add the third light/dark/light (★light/medium/light) segment. The nine-patch should measure 1⅝″x 1⅝″ and its center square should measure ⅜″ × ⅜″. Trim the seams.

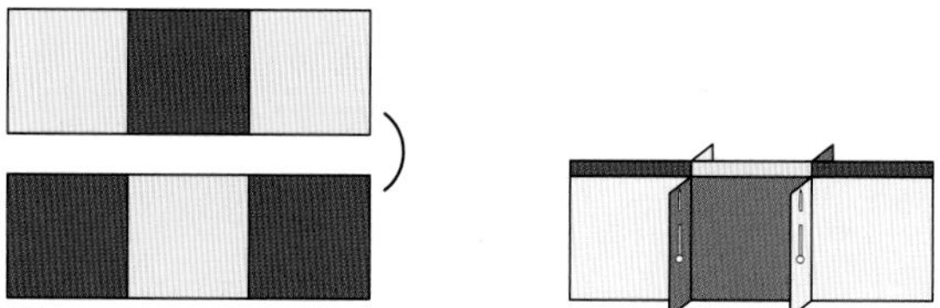
Pin and sew.

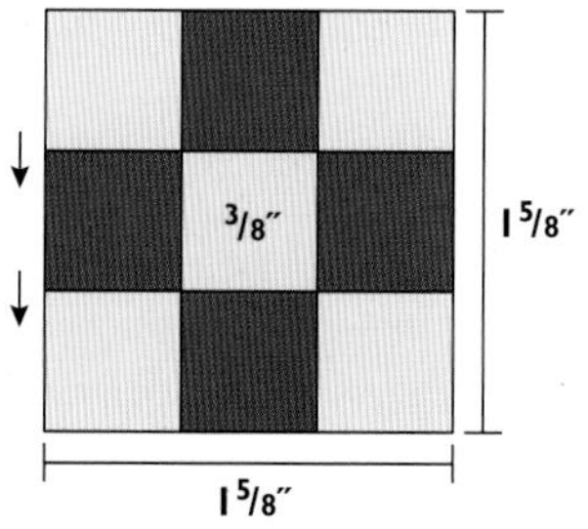
⅜″
1⅝″
1⅝″
Completed nine-patch

Shape C Rail Construction

1. Sew 1 strip unit of medium/light/medium. Press after adding each strip and measure. Two strips sewn should measure $1\frac{1}{4}''$ from edge to edge and 3 strips sewn should measure $1\frac{5}{8}''$ from edge to edge. Press the seams in one direction and trim.

2. From the strip unit, cut 4 segments $1\frac{5}{8}''$ wide.

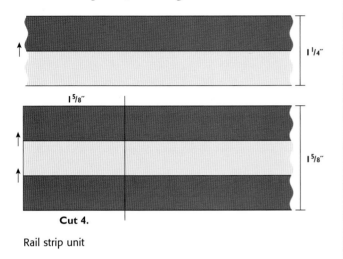

Cut 4.

Rail strip unit

Pieced Block Construction

1. Lay out all block elements.

2. Construct the nine-patch/rail unit by joining the units into rows, then the rows into the completed nine-patch/rail unit. Two rows should measure $2\frac{3}{4}'' \times 3\frac{7}{8}''$ and the complete unit should measure $3\frac{7}{8}'' \times 3\frac{7}{8}''$ unfinished.

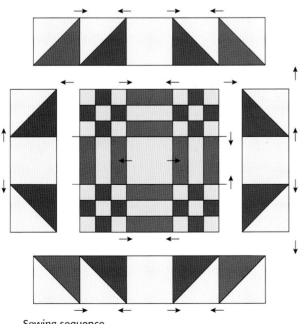

Sewing sequence

3. Complete the block construction as shown. The block measures $6\frac{1}{8}'' \times 6\frac{1}{8}''$ unfinished. Make 5 (4 corner blocks as shown and 1 center block with different fabric placement).

Background Construction

The background is constructed from 16 squares, 4 quarter-square triangle units, and 5 Goose in the Pond blocks, creating a 5×5 grid of squares.

Noteworthy

The quarter-square triangle units are not oversized and custom cut.

- Cut 16 squares $6\frac{1}{8}'' \times 6\frac{1}{8}''$ from the primary background fabric.
- Cut 3 squares $6\frac{7}{8}'' \times 6\frac{7}{8}''$ from the primary background fabric; cut into quarters diagonally.
- Cut 1 square $6\frac{7}{8}'' \times 6\frac{7}{8}''$ from the third background fabric; cut into quarters diagonally.

(If you did not change the background fabric of the center block you will not need any quarter-square triangle units, and you will need 20 instead of 16 squares $6\frac{1}{8}'' \times 6\frac{1}{8}''$ of primary background.)

Quarter-Square Triangle Units

1. Lay out 3 triangles from the primary background fabric and 1 from the third background fabric. Join the 4 triangles into a $6\frac{1}{8}'' \times 6\frac{1}{8}''$ unfinished square, referring to Quarter-Square Triangle Units (page 43). Make 4.

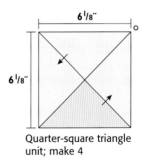

Quarter-square triangle unit; make 4

2. Lay out the 5 Goose in the Pond blocks, the plain squares, and the quarter-square triangle units. Join the blocks, squares, and quarter-square triangle units into rows and the rows into the completed pieced

background. Press all the seams open. The background measures 28⅝″ × 28⅝″ unfinished.

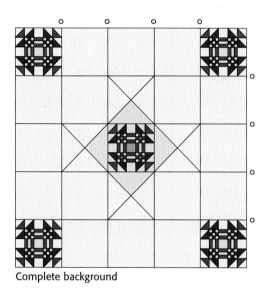

Complete background

Borders

Curved Border Design Element

This appliqué element will be constructed from 3 shapes that are appliquéd to each other off-site to make 1 single unit. Make 4. Each curved border design element is then inserted into the seam when joining the first border to the quilt top. The outward-curved turned-under edge remains unattached until the borders are added, then that edge is appliquéd in place by hand or machine (use your favorite method).

This curved design element consists of 3 separate shapes: D—primary background, E—pink, and F—dark magenta. Refer to Appliqué (page 54) for shape preparation. Each pattern shape reflects one-half the shape and includes a ¼″ seam allowance at the bottom straight edge. Arrows point toward the edge where the seam allowance goes under the shape on top.

1. Trace each half D, E, and F shape (page 87) onto a separate piece of white paper. Create a dark, clear image, transferring all arrows, lines, and letters. Turn the paper over and retrace, using a light box if needed.

2. Place the right-sided image of D, right side up, on a light box and secure it with painter's tape.

3. Layer 2 pieces of freezer paper together, shiny side to dull side, slightly larger than the size of a complete D shape. Iron the sheets together smoothly to eliminate wrinkles. Place the freezer paper over the half-D white paper shape, shiny side down, and trace exactly, transferring all arrows, lines, and letters. Remove the freezer paper and turn the half-D white paper shape over and re-secure. Place the freezer paper over the half-D shape again, shiny side down, matching up the dotted center-lines and making sure the bottom seam allowance line is straight. Trace as you did before, transferring all markings and creating the whole shape D. Repeat this process for E and F. These 3 freezer-paper templates will be reused to make all 4 curved border designs.

4. Cut out each freezer-paper shape (D, E, and F) on the lines, including the ¼″ seam allowance at the bottom of the shape.

5. Press each whole freezer-paper shape, shiny side down, onto the wrong side of the appropriate fabric.

6. Cut around each freezer-paper shape, leaving a ³⁄₁₆″–¼″ seam allowance on all curved edges only. Cut along the bottom straight edge exactly, which includes a ¼″ seam allowance for sewing in the seam later. Refer to Appliqué (page 54) for the preparation of the shapes and the removal of the paper.

7. To know exactly where one shape aligns onto the next, lay the removed freezer-paper templates for E and F on the right side of the fabric shapes and trace along the arrowed paper edge with a removable marking tool.

8. Place shape E onto shape F, using the drawn line as a placement guide and making sure the bottom edges continue in a straight line. Lightly glue baste in place, then appliqué E to F by hand or machine.

9. Place shape D onto E/F similarly. Using the existing freezer-paper templates, make 3 more curved border design elements.

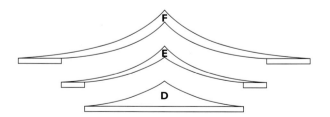

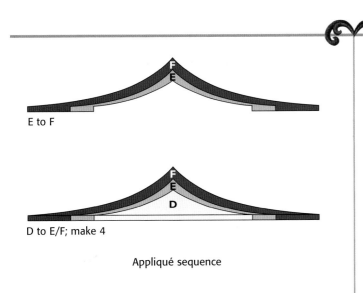

E to F

D to E/F; make 4

Appliqué sequence

Boxed-Corner Border

- Cut 2 strips 2½″ × 28⅝″ from the secondary background fabric for the sides.
- Cut 2 strips 2½″ × 32⅝″ from the secondary background fabric for the top and bottom.

1. With the quilt top right side up, place 1 curved design element on 1 side, right sides together, matching and pinning the centers and ends. (The curved element will be ¼″ from the quilt top corners.)

Position curved border design element.

2. Place 1 side border face down over the curved design element, aligning and matching the centers and quilt corners. Remove the pins from underneath and secure all 3 layers at the centers and corners; add additional pins for stable sewing. Sew and press the seam open. The design-element seam presses toward the center of the quilt. Repeat for the opposite side.

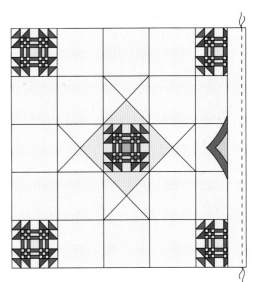

Position and sew the boxed-corner border in place.

3. Add the top and bottom curved design elements and border. Be sure to center the design element so it lies within the space between the 2 side border seams. Press the seams open. The quilt top measures 32⅝″ × 32⅝″ from the straight border edges.

Add remaining borders.

Checkerboard Border

⅜″ grid dimension

This border incorporates a checkerboard that gives the same feeling as the nine-patches and creates repetition and continuity of design. Also, because the checkerboard design travels under the curved design element, a significant number of squares would be hidden and create bulk. To prevent that, I inserted a rectangle of primary background between 2 sections of checkerboard where that occurs.

Refer to Creating Straight Strip Units (page 47).

- Cut 4 rectangles 1¼″ × 2⅝″ of primary background fabric.

- Cut 8 strips ⅞″ × 40″ each of dark purple and third background (light) fabric.

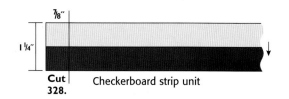

Cut 328.   Checkerboard strip unit

1. Sew a light and a dark strip together. Make 8. Press toward the dark. The unit measures 1¼″ from edge to edge. Trim the seam.

2. Cut 328 segments ⅞″.

3. Sew 40 segments together for the sides. Make 4. Measure as you sew (pages 25–26), press the seams in one direction, and trim the seams.

4. Sew 42 segments together for the top and bottom. Make 4.

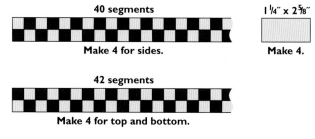

40 segments
Make 4 for sides.

1¼″ × 2⅝″
Make 4.

42 segments
Make 4 for top and bottom.

Checkerboards

5. Join a 1¼″ × 2⅝″ rectangle between two 40-segment units. Make 2. Press toward the rectangle.

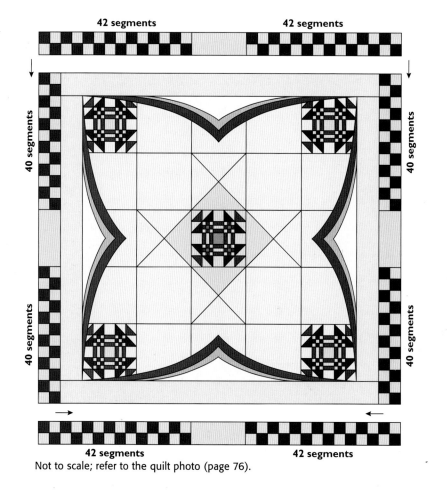

42 segments   42 segments

40 segments   40 segments

40 segments   40 segments

42 segments   42 segments

Not to scale; refer to the quilt photo (page 76).

6. Add to the sides of the quilt, moving the loose edge of the curved design element out of the way. Press toward the quilt.

7. Join a 1¼″ × 2⅝″ rectangle between two 42-segment units. Make 2. Press toward the rectangle.

8. Add to the top and bottom of the quilt. Press toward the quilt. The quilt top measures 34⅛″ × 34⅛″ from the checkerboard edges.

Sawtooth Border

1⅛″ grid dimension

This border echoes the half-square triangle element of the blocks and serves to create repetition and continuity in the design. This border also travels under the design element, so I again added a rectangle of background fabric between 2 sawtooth sections to eliminate bulk, but more importantly to clarify the point of the curved design element. Part of this rectangle will show in the quilt, so it is important to make it from the background fabric. When working with sawtooth designs, be sure to recognize the importance of the diagonal seam and its direction when joining individual units together.

- Cut 4 rectangles 1⅝″ × 4⅞″ from primary background fabric.

- Cut 4 strips 2¼″ × 40″ each of primary background fabric (light) and medium magenta. Subcut into 54 squares of each color 2¼″ × 2¼″; cut in half diagonally.

1. Join a light and a medium triangle together and press toward the dark. Custom cut a square 1⅝″ × 1⅝″ from each. Make 108. Refer to Individual Half-Square Triangles (page 40) and Oversize and Custom-Cut Technique (page 40).

Noteworthy

When adding the sawtooth border, you will be matching every third checkerboard seam to a sawtooth seam, so it is important to press the seams in opposite directions and to sew accurately.

Three checker-boards for one sawtooth

2. Join 13 sawtooth units together. Make 4 (2 with the diagonal seams in one direction and 2 with the diagonal seams in the opposite direction) for the sides and

press in the opposite direction of the checkerboard border.

3. Join a background rectangle between two 13-sawtooth units. Make 2. Press toward the rectangle.

4. Join 14 sawtooth units together. Make 4 (2 with the diagonal seams in one direction and 2 with the diagonal seams in the opposite direction) for the top and bottom and press in the opposite direction of the checkerboard border.

5. Join a background rectangle between two 14-sawtooth units and press toward the rectangle. Make 2.

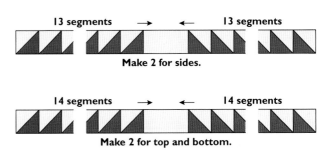

13 segments → ← 13 segments

Make 2 for sides.

14 segments → ← 14 segments

Make 2 for top and bottom.

Press seams opposite of checkerboard border.

6. Add the 2 side borders to the quilt top, moving the curved design out of the way as you did when adding the checkerboard. Press toward the sawtooth border.

7. Add the 2 remaining borders to the top and bottom of the quilt. Press toward the sawtooth border. The quilt top measures 36⅜″ × 36⅜″ unfinished.

Final Plain Borders

The next 5 borders are added to the quilt separately, using the partial-seam corner style.

- Border 1 finishes to ⅛″ (see Very Narrow (⅛″) Borders, page 53). Cut 4 strips 1″ × 36⅞″ of blue accent.

- Border 2 finishes to ¾″ (this border follows the ⅛″ border; see Very Narrow (⅛″) Borders, page 53). Cut 4 strips 1⅝″ × 37⅝″ of primary background fabric.

- Border 3 finishes to 1¾″. Cut 4 strips 2¼″ × 39⅞″ on the cross grain of dark purple.

- Border 4 finishes to 1⅛″. Cut 4 strips 1⅝″ × 42¾″ on the length grain of secondary background fabric.

- Border 5 finishes to 3⅞″. Cut 4 strips 4⅜″ × 47¾″ on the length grain of dark magenta.

Add each set of borders as illustrated. The quilt top measures 51⅝″ × 51⅝″ unfinished.

Partial-seam corner technique; add each plain border the same way.

Center Appliqué Design

The center appliqué design is created in quadrants consisting of 3 units each. Assemble 4 of each unit, then appliqué to the background. Creating depth and shadows is important to the visual design and requires clear value contrast between 2 touching shapes. I chose just 2 colors, purple (1 very dark, 1 medium) and magenta (1 very dark, 1 medium, 1 pink). The very darks appear solid and the medium and pink have some visual texture but are tone-on-tone in style. This creates a smooth, quiet appearance and helps delineate between the touching values.

One quadrant, 3 units

Prepare 1 set of paper templates for the 3 units and use those to create all 4 sets. Label the shapes with letters, starting with G and working from the background up. The arrows point to the edge where the seam allowance goes under the shape on top. Dashed lines indicate the continuation of a template shape under another. A red line indicates where to snip the seam allowance and reverse whatever you did to the seam allowance before the red line. This occurs in unit 1 between shapes G and L, and unit 3 between shapes O and P. The arrows will determine what reverse action to take. This snipping of the seam allowance allows shapes to interlock (over/under) along one edge.

Unit 1 is made up of 2 subunits of 3 shapes each (subunit 1: shapes G/H/I, subunit 2: shapes J/K/L), which are joined together to create 1 unit. Of the shapes G through L that make up unit 1, 4 (shapes G, H, J, and K) require reverse shapes. This unit, although not complicated to create, has the most pieces and reverses.

Unit 2 is made up of 2 shapes, M and N.

Unit 3 is made up of 2 shapes, O and P, and their reverses, Or and Pr.

Freezer-Paper Templates

1. Trace shapes I, L, M, and N onto separate pieces of plain white paper. Create a dark, clear image, transferring all information. Turn each paper over and retrace, using a light box if needed.

2. Place the left side of shape I right side up on a light box and secure with painter's tape. Layer 2 pieces of freezer paper together, shiny side to dull side, slightly larger than the complete shape I. Iron the freezer paper smooth to prevent wrinkles. Place the freezer paper over the image, shiny side down, and trace, transferring all information.

3. Remove the freezer paper, turn the white paper over, and re-secure and place the freezer paper over shape I again, joining the mirror image at the dashed line for exact placement. Trace, creating the whole shape I on the layered freezer paper.

4. Repeat Steps 1–3 for shapes L, M, and N.

5. Trace shapes G, H, J, K, O, and P directly onto the dull side of 2 layers of freezer paper, transferring all information. Leave some space between the shapes to maneuver your scissors.

6. Cut out shapes G through P from the 2 layers of freezer paper, exactly on the lines.

7. Take shapes G, H, J, K, O, and P and turn them over and trace them onto the dull side of 2 layers of freezer paper. Label them Gr, Hr, and so on, and transfer all information.

8. Cut out shapes Gr, Hr, Jr, Kr, Or, and Pr from the 2 layers of freezer paper, exactly on the line. You now have 16 reusable templates to create all 3 units. You will use each one 4 times to create the entire center design.

Building the Quadrants

I suggest that you build 1 unit at a time to see how it all works. Once you have 1 quadrant (unit 1/2/3) of the design completed, you can build the other 3 quadrants in a more production-line fashion if you choose.

UNIT 1

Shapes G–Gr, H–Hr, I, J–Jr, K–Kr, L

1. Place each freezer-paper template, shiny side down, on the wrong side of the appropriate fabric and press to adhere. Cut around each shape, allowing a ¼˝ seam allowance on all edges.

2. Refer to Appliqué (page 54) for information on turning edges and removing the freezer-paper template. Notice the red line on shape G, which indicates where the seam allowance is snipped and the treatment of seam allowance changes.

3. On shapes G–Gr, H–Hr, and I, lay the freezer-paper template on the right side of the fabric shape and trace a line on the fabric along the arrowed edge of the paper as a placement guide for the next shape to be positioned.

4. Position and glue baste shapes G–Gr and H–Hr under shape I, keeping glue away from the edges to be appliquéd. Set aside.

5. On shapes J–Jr and K–Kr, lay the freezer-paper template over the fabric shape and mark a placement line as you did previously.

6. Position and glue baste J–Jr and K–Kr under shape L.

7. Position and glue baste subunit J–Jr/K–Kr/L onto subunit G–Gr/H–Hr/I along the placement lines exactly. All edges should be turned under. Appliqué all glue-basted edges by hand or machine. Make 4. Set aside.

UNIT 2

Shapes M and N; no red line

1. Repeat Steps 1 and 2 for unit 1.

2. On shape M, lay the freezer-paper template on the right side of the fabric shape M and trace a line on the fabric along the arrowed edge as a placement guide for shape N.

3. Position and glue baste shape M under shape N. All edges should be turned under. Appliqué all glue-basted edges by hand or machine. Make 4. Set aside.

UNIT 3

Shapes O and P

1. Repeat Steps 1 and 2 for unit 1 and notice the red line on both shapes that indicates where the seam allowance treatment reverses to allow those 2 shapes to interlock.

2. Lay the paper template on the right side of the fabric shape and trace a line on the fabric along the arrowed edges on both shapes. Position and glue baste shapes O and P over/under each other. All edges should be turned under. Appliqué all glue-basted edges by hand or machine. Make 4.

Appliqué to Background

Using the quilt photo and paying attention to the grid/seamlines of the background, glue baste each quadrant in place and appliqué. The quilt top is complete.

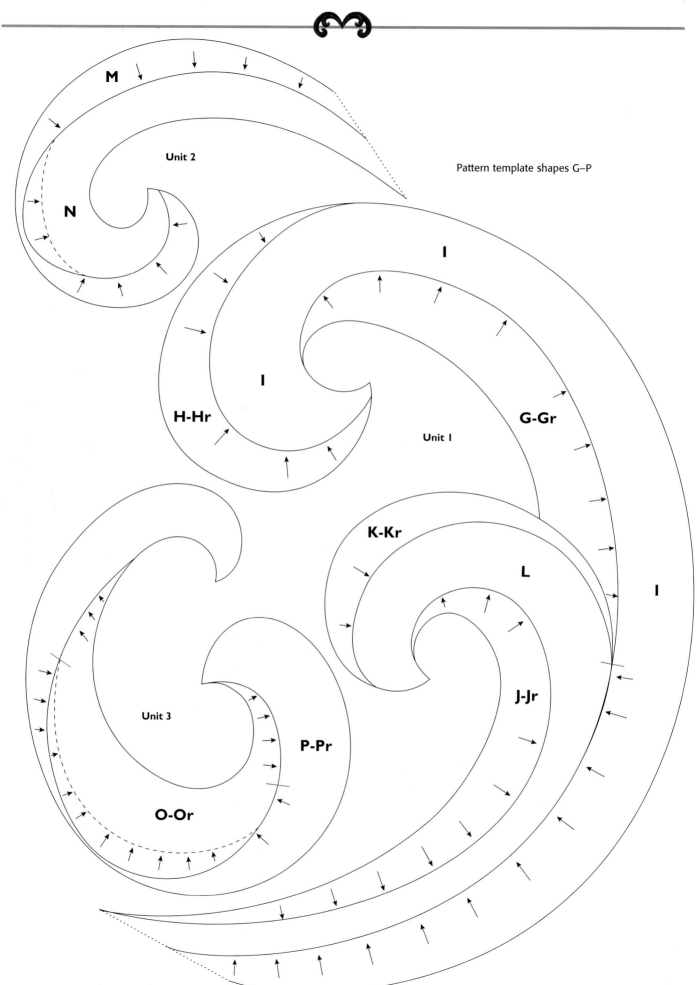

Pattern template shapes G–P

M

Unit 2

N

I

I

H-Hr

Unit I

G-Gr

K-Kr

L

I

J-Jr

Unit 3

P-Pr

O-Or

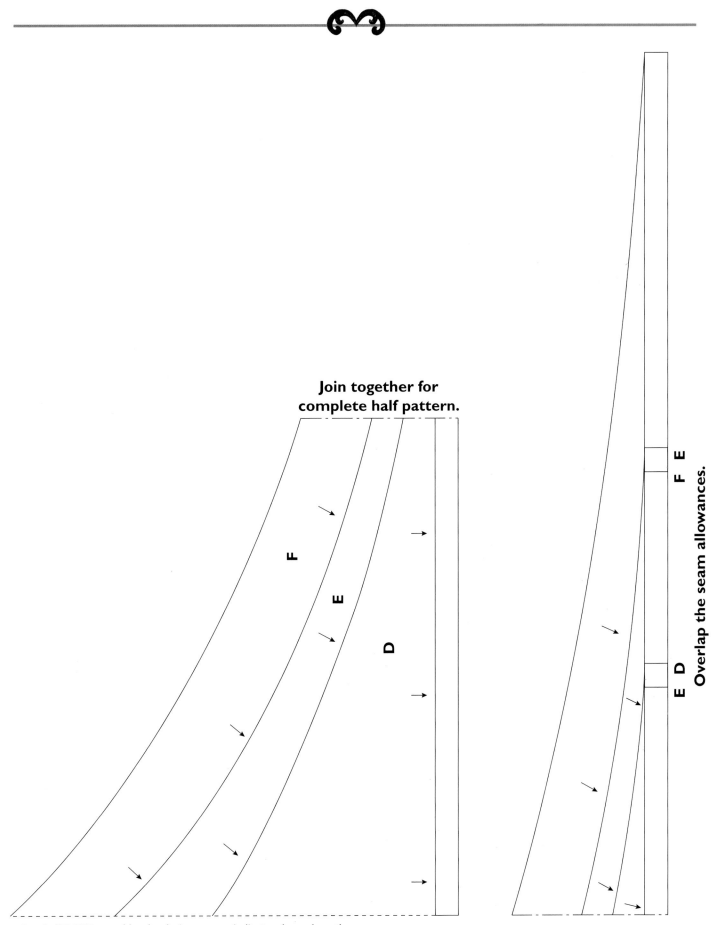

Join together for complete half pattern.

F

E

D

Overlap the seam allowances.

F E

E D

One-half D/E/F curved border design; arrows indicate edges where the seam allowance goes under the shape on top.

Petite Sirah

42″ × 42″ unfinished

Designed, machine pieced, and hand appliquéd by author, machine
quilted by author and Jill Schumacher, Rio Vista, CA

Color

I did not have a palette fabric or inspiration object to develop the color for this quilt. I chose nine different colors, one for each plate (pink, magenta, purple, blue, turquoise, bright pink, ocean blue, orange, and yellow). I expanded each color by choosing seven more variations because I wanted a variety of visual textures with subtle value changes to create a smoothness to each plate, using each fabric twice. The leaf fabrics are different for each plate, which contributes to the smoothness. The dark red and purple backgrounds create a dramatic richness that shows off and complements each plate color. The curved frame fabric, a light value of the purple, works beautifully. The secondary design colors were easy to choose by repeating the green and dark red, and the orange accent always works with purple. The first border repeats the colors of the curved frame and the secondary design, while the chain-of-squares border and the ¼″ border repeat the plate colors. The final purple border completes the quilt.

Design

Petite Sirah, a combination of piecing and appliqué, blends traditional and contemporary styles. The curved frames are an idea I've wanted to try for a long time, so this seemed to be the perfect opportunity to incorporate them into a quilt. Having a couple of ideas and then following basic design principles helps transform ideas into reality. My initial idea was to add leaves to each plate to create flowers, then frame them with the curved design. Because I like to balance curves with straight lines, I added the corner piecing on each block, which creates a secondary design of squares on point. The zigzag/curved frame border relates to elements already used. The chain-of-squares border was chosen to enhance the secondary corner design created by the blocks.

Vital Statistics:
- Block Size: 7¼″ × 7¼″ unfinished
- Drafting Category: Miscellaneous (16 equal division of a circle, 22.5° each)
- Number of Shapes: 2
- Number of Pieces: 17

Techniques Used: appliqué (page 54), templates (page 31), rotary cutting (page 30), creating straight strip units (page 47), Y-seams (page 46), and very narrow (⅛″) borders (page 53) Matching seams, same direction (page 49)

Fabric Requirements

- Plates and Chain-of-Squares Border: 6″ × 6″ squares of 8 different fabrics in 9 different colors
- Background 1 (Plate Backgrounds, Zigzag Border, Secondary Corner Design, Chain-of-Squares Border and Spacer Border 1): 1¾ yards of dark red★
- Background 2 (Block, Zigzag Border, and Final Border 3): 2⅜ yards of dark purple★
- Curved Frame: ⅜ yard of light mauve★
- Accent Border 2: ⅛ yard of yellow
- Leaves: 6″ × 6″ squares of 9 different greens
- Zigzag Border and Secondary Corner Design: ⅝ yard of accent green
- Zigzag Border, Secondary Corner Design, Chain-of-Squares Border: ½ yard of accent orange
- Embroidery floss for leaf stems

★Place the plates on different background fabric candidates until you find the one perfect fabric that shows off all the plate colors the best. This is background 1. Then choose another fabric of the same value in the same color family, perhaps a neighboring color on the color wheel. This is background 2. Now choose a fabric for the curved frame that contrasts with the fabric it will touch; you want to clearly see the frame.

Dresden Plate Blocks

Make a template for shape A (page 31), which includes ¼″ seam allowances, and shape B, for which no seam allowances are needed (page 98).

Instructions to make 1 Dresden Plate:
- Shape A: Cut 2 each from 8 different fabrics (16 total).
- Shape B: Create 1 freezer-paper shape that can be used 9 times for all block centers (see Appliqué, page 54).

1. Fold 1 shape A in half lengthwise, right sides together; align edges exactly and finger-press well. Sew across the wide end, from the raw edges to the fold, with a small stitch length.

2. Trim the seam allowance to a generous ⅛″, trim the point, and turn shape A right side out, carefully using a blunted toothpick or similar tool to extend the point. Manipulate the shape so it is symmetrical and press. The point and seam should be in line with the finger-pressed fold. Make 16.

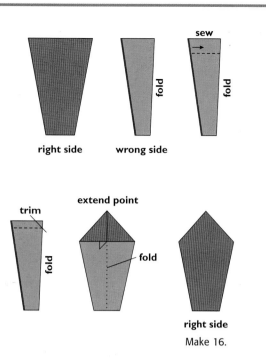

right side   **wrong side**

extend point

trim

fold

fold

right side
Make 16.

Creating one shape A

3. Lay out the 16 A shapes in a circle, in the order you choose.

4. Align 2 adjacent A shapes on top of each other accurately and sew as shown. Repeat for the next 2 A shapes. Do not press or trim the seam allowances until the plate is complete. All seam allowances should be left free.

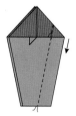

Make 8 pairs.

Noteworthy

To eliminate thread tails at the beginning of the sewn edge, begin sewing 2 stitches in from the edge, backstitch to the edge, and then continue forward. Be sure you are always sewing the correct edges so you do not get your petals out of position.

5. Sew 2 pairs together to make one-quarter of the circle, continuing to align the edges and seams. Place the shape A template over the 2 inside seams to check for accuracy and symmetry. Create 3 more quarters.

6. Sew 2 adjacent quarters together. Make 2. Continue to monitor accuracy with the template shape A.

7. Sew the 2 halves together in 2 seams. There should be a hole in the center.

8. Evaluate carefully and press all the seams in one direction. Make 9. Do not trim the seams yet.

Blocking the Dresden Plate Blocks

The sewn plate probably looks like a cone at this point—not at all flat—and you're thinking that you've done something wrong. Not to worry! Don't panic as I did. The plate will need to be blocked to lie nice and flat and become the correct size. Do this carefully and patiently.

1. Steam press a 6″ × 6″ square of freezer paper onto your ironing-board cover. This will preshrink the freezer paper.

2. Carefully pull up the square and trace the blocking pattern on the dull side. With a dry iron, re-press the freezer paper onto the ironing board. You should be able to use this to block a minimum of 3 times.

3. Spritz the fabric plate with water to dampen it; do not soak it.

4. Place the fabric plate onto the tracing and begin blocking by pinning the fabric points to the paper points.

5. Work opposite points across the plate, keeping seams aligned, encouraging the plate flat with your hands. Do not pin at the very ends of the points and risk tearing the fabric; place the pins slightly in from the point. Use very fine (.4mm) pins and position them flat so you can place the iron on top and press the plate dry. Continue to spritz as needed to manipulate the plate. Place a book over it while it is cooling so it will become familiar with being flat. Once the plate is blocked and it meets your standards, trim the seam allowances. Good-quality 100% cotton is easily manipulated into a flat Dresden Plate.

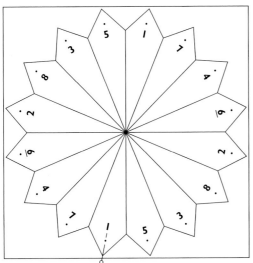

Blocking pattern; numbers indicate pinning
sequence; • indicates pin placement

Center Circles

Choose a center fabric for each plate and refer to
Appliqué (page 54) to prepare the center fabric circles.
Appliqué the centers in place. Do not cut out the back
fabric. Make 9.

Preparing Background Blocks

Curved Frame: Make a plastic template (page 31) for
shape C (page 98), transferring all lines. Notice that the
bottom straight edge includes a ¼″ seam allowance. You
need a total of 64 curved frame shapes: 36 for the blocks
and 28 for the zigzag border. Refer to Appliqué (page
54). Trace and cut out 7 shape Cs onto the dull side of
the double-layered freezer paper. You can use each shape
10 times.

Background Block Assembly: These blocks will be
created larger and trimmed to the correct size after the
plates, leaves, and embroidery have been added.

Instructions to make 9 blocks:

• Cut 9 squares 5″ × 5″ from background 1.

• Cut 6 strips 2″ × 40″ from background 2.

Subcut 4 strips into 18 rectangles 8″ long; you will
have extra of the fourth strip. Subcut the remaining strips
into 18 rectangles 5″ long.

1. On the right side of all nine 5″ × 5″ squares, mark the
center of all sides at the edge.

2. On the wrong side of each curved frame shape, mark
the center on the raw edge.

3. Align a curved frame onto 1 block, right sides together;
match and pin the centers, keeping the edges aligned.

4. Align a 2″ × 5″ rectangle over the curved frame, right
side down. Pin at the center and ends to hold all 3
layers in place. Sew and press the seam open (there are
3 seam allowances in this seam; the curved frame seam
allowance presses toward the block). Repeat for the
opposite side. The curved edge of the frame now lies
right side up on the added rectangle.

5. Align a curved frame onto a third side of the 5″ square,
right sides together, matching and pinning the center.
Check to be sure the curved frame fits within the 2
side seams; adjust if necessary.

6. Align a 2″ × 8″ rectangle over the curved frame, right
side down, and pin in place. Press as you did for the
sides and repeat for the fourth side. Make 9. All blocks
measure 8″ × 8″ unfinished.

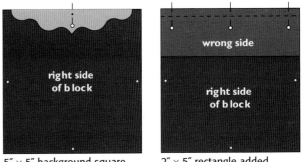

5″ × 5″ background square
and curved frame

2″ × 5″ rectangle added

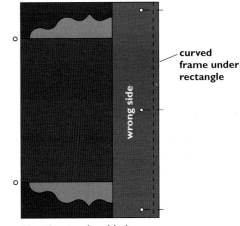

curved
frame under
rectangle

2″ × 8″ rectangle added

7. Press each block from the back. Glue baste the curved edge in place by slightly lifting the edge and placing a thin line of glue far enough away from the edge so you won't appliqué through it.

8. Appliqué the 36 curved edges in place. Do not cut away the back fabric.

Appliquéing the Dresden Plates onto Framed Background Blocks

1. With a ruler and a marker that you can see and is removable, draw lines on the inside square from corner to corner, then vertically and horizontally at the midpoint. These lines will help you place the plate, leaves, and embroidery. I use a white Clover pen.

Noteworthy

Regardless of the marking tool you use, do not press this block again until all appliqué and embroidery are complete.

2. Now place the background block over the placement guide (if using a dark fabric, a light box will be needed) and mark the leaf placement reference lines for one-quarter of the design and rotate for the remainder of the design.

Placement guide for plates, leaves, and curved frames; one quadrant of actual finished size of block (not to be used for templates)

3. Place 1 marked background block on your ironing board. Take 1 plate and push a pin through the center of the center B circle. Now push the pin through the center of the background block and into the ironing board so the pin is vertical and the plate is capable of spinning around the pin.

4. Position the plate as best you can as diagramed. Ideally, the plate seams fall on the marked lines.

5. Once the plate is positioned properly, glue baste it in place, well away from the edge to be appliquéd. Use a small amount of glue.

6. Appliqué around the edge of the plate points. Do not cut away the background.

Leaves

1. Choose 9 different green fabrics, 1 for each plate. You will need a total of 216 leaves, 24 for each plate. Create 24 freezer-paper leaf shapes to create all 216 leaves. Refer to Appliqué (page 54) for preparation details.

2. Glue baste all 24 leaves onto 1 block (you will need only a couple of dots of glue) and appliqué them in place. Make 9 blocks.

3. Embroider the stems with a single strand of DMC embroidery thread.

4. Remove the white Clover pen markings with the point of the iron. Read the marker manufacturer's instructions to remove other types of markings. Place the blocks face down on a soft surface and press well.

Trimming Blocks to Correct Size

Noteworthy

Following the rule of measure twice, cut once, I suggest that you draw lines (with a removable marking tool) and measure them before cutting. If your blocks do not measure 8″ × 8″ at the outset, make the appropriate adjustment. You must end up with blocks that are 7¼″ × 7¼″ unfinished.

1. With 1 block facing right side up on your rotary cutting mat, align the ruler so the 1⅜″ line of the ruler is over the last seam sewn and the 3⅝″ line runs through the center of the block vertically. Trim the excess (⅜″).

Repeat for the other side. The block measures 7¼″ wide unfinished.

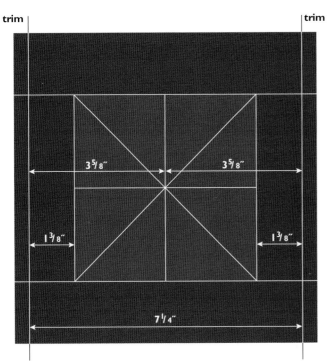

Trim first 2 sides.

2. Repeat the Step 1 trimming process for the remaining 2 sides. The block measures 7¼″ × 7¼″ unfinished. Trim 9 blocks.

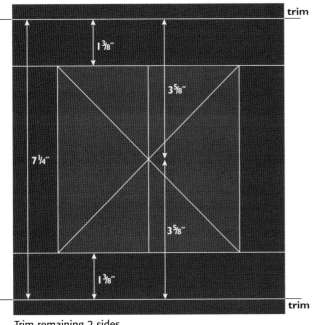

Trim remaining 2 sides.

Secondary Corner Design

On each corner of each block you will add a triangle cut from a strip unit consisting of 3 fabrics. See Very Narrow (⅛″) Borders (page 53) and Creating Straight Strip Units (page 47). I used the dark red background 1 fabric, accent green, and accent orange for the strip unit. Choose a color for the ⅛″ strip that clearly contrasts with the other 2 fabrics to be effective.

Make a template for shape D (page 98), transferring all lines and extending them out into the seam allowance area. See Accurate Templates (page 31). Make a second template for shape E (page 98), which is the placement guide for shape D. Do not add seam allowances to shape E.

Noteworthy

If you double-blunt the extended points of template D (page 32), the edges of the fabric will align with the block edges for easy, accurate placement.

Strip Unit

- Cut 5 strips 1″ × 40″ of accent green for fabric strip 1.
- Cut 5 strips 1″ × 40″ of accent orange for fabric strip 2 (this will be the eventual ⅛″ strip).
- Cut 5 strips 1½″ × 40″ of dark red for fabric strip 3.

   Instructions to make 1 strip unit:

1. Sew strip 1 to 2, trim the ¼″ seam allowance to an exact ⅛″, and press toward strip 2.

2. Sew strips 1/2 to strip 3, with strip 3 on the bottom; align the edges of strip 3 and 2, but sew next to the just-trimmed seam allowance edge.

3. Evaluate, trim the excess seam allowance to a generous ⅛″, and press toward strip 3. Make 5.

4. Cut 64 shape D triangles from the strip units, always aligning the lines on the template with the seamlines. Be sure you have placed the template on the strip unit correctly so you do not get your colors out of position. Set aside.

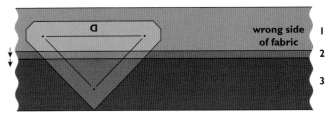

Cut 64 shape Ds from strip units.

Adding the Secondary Corner Design

1. On 1 block, right side up, position the shape E placement guide triangle over each corner and mark a line across the top of the template.

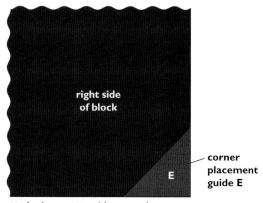

right side of block

corner placement guide E

E

Mark placement guide on each corner.

2. Using the marked line as a reference, position a pieced D triangle, face down, against the marked line and pin in place.

3. Sew the triangle onto the block corner and bring the corner of the triangle over the stitching to meet the block's corner. If it meets well, trim the seam allowance of the triangle only (leave the block corner in place), bring the corners together again, and press. I do not trim out the block corner. Repeat for the remaining 3 corners. Repeat for the remaining 8 blocks.

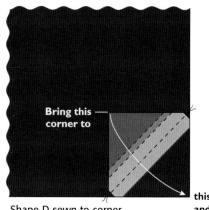

Bring this corner to

this corner and press.

Shape D sewn to corner

Shape D pressed in place

4. Lay out the 9 blocks in a pleasing arrangement. Sew the blocks into rows and the rows into the completed quilt top, matching the seams of the corner triangles. Refer to Matching Seams Same Direction (page 49). Press all the seams open. The quilt top measures 20¾″ × 20¾″ unfinished.

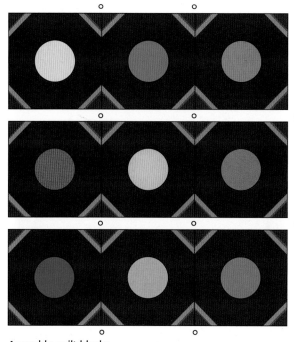

Assemble quilt blocks.

Pieced Zigzag Border

This border repeats the shapes, colors, and fabrics of the background, curved frame, and secondary corner design. You will create 12 pieced, appliquéd, and Y-seamed units for the 4 sides, and 4 pieced and appliquéd corner units.

Make templates for shapes F, G, H, I, J, K, L, M, and N, (page 99). Refer to Y-Seam Construction (page 46).

Noteworthy

You already have 28 shape C curved frames. Place and pin the C curved frame in the seam between F/G and F/Gr for the sides and between F/K as in the Dresden Plate blocks on page 91. Shapes K, G, and Gr reflect correct placement of the shape C curved frame.

Side and Corner Units

- Shape F: Cut 24 for side units.

- Shapes G, Gr, H, Hr, I, Ir, and J: Cut 12 each for side units.

- Shapes F, K, L, M, and N: Cut 4 each for corner units.

SIDE UNIT ASSEMBLY

1. Create 12 F/C/G/H/I units and 12 F/C/Gr/Hr/Ir units.

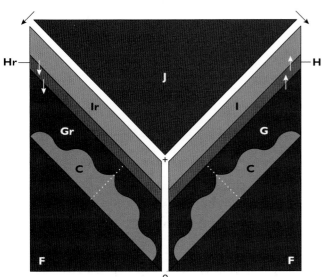

Zigzag side border unit. Make 12.

2. Join 1 F/C/G/H/I and 1 F/C/Gr/Hr/Ir unit. Sew from the F end to the I–Ir dot and backstitch. Make 12.

3. Insert a J triangle shape into an F/C/G/H/I/F/ C/Gr/Hr/Ir unit, sewing from the outside edge to the dot and backstitching. This means shape J will be on top for one seam and on the bottom for the second seam. Make 12.

CORNER UNIT ASSEMBLY

Create 4 F/C/K/L/M/N units.

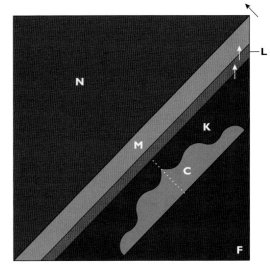

Zigzag corner unit; make 4

ADDING THE SECONDARY CORNER DESIGN

1. Use the shape E placement guide to align and join a shape D triangle to each shape F of the 12 side border units and one shape D triangle to each corner border unit.

2. Join 3 side border units. Make 2. Add to the sides of the quilt, matching all seams, and press all the seams open.

3. Join 3 side border units. Make 2. Add a corner unit to each end of both. Press all the seams open. Add to the top and bottom of the quilt. Press all the seams open. The quilt top measures 33″ × 33″ unfinished.

Chain-of-Squares Border

Make a template for shapes O and P (page 99).
- Shape O: Cut 22 each from a variety of 8 plate colors (you will be repeating fabrics) for a total of 176, which includes the 4 corners. I used the yellow center plate color for a plain-fabric border because that color drew too much attention when used in the chain of squares.

- Shape P: Cut 360 of dark red (background 1).

I planned my color order before starting to sew. I arranged the warm colors together and the cool colors together. I tried to keep plate and border colors near each other as best I could.

Chain-of-Squares Border Assembly

1. Following the color plan, start with the right side and create 1 border at a time. Working clockwise, join 43 shape Os to 86 shape Ps (page 97). Trim the seams.

Make 176 units total, 22 of each color.

2. Join the 43 P/O/P units together, press the seams open, and trim the seams.

3. Add a P triangle to each end of the P/O/P border and trim ¼″ from the point of the square.

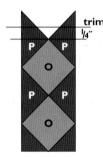

Trim both ends of each border.

4. Repeat Steps 1, 2, and 3 to make the 3 remaining borders: bottom border (44 Os, 90 Ps), left side border (44 Os, 90 Ps), and top border (45 Os, 92 Ps).

5. Add each border clockwise around the quilt, pinning well to keep the pieced border from shifting. Sew with the border on top. Press the seams toward the quilt. The quilt top measures 34½″ × 34½″ unfinished.

Three Plain-Fabric Borders

The next 3 borders are all added in a boxed-corner fashion, meaning that the side borders are added first, and then the top and bottom borders are added.

Spacer Border 1

This border is added to separate the chain-of-squares border from the yellow border. It adds viewing clarification and floats the design by using the same fabric used for shape P.
- Cut 2 strips 1″ × 34½″; add to the sides.
- Cut 2 strips 1″ × 35½″; add to the top and bottom.

The quilt top measures 35½″ × 35½″ unfinished.

Accent Border 2

I chose to use the ninth plate color in this position because using yellow in the chain-of-squares border was visually too disruptive and demanding.
- Cut 2 strips ¾″ × 35½″; add to the sides.
- Cut 2 strips ¾″ × 36″; add to the top and bottom.

The quilt top measures 36″ × 36″ unfinished.

Final Border 3

I cut the final border slightly wider (1″), so I can square the quilt before binding.
- Cut 2 length-grain strips 3½″ × 36″; add to the sides.
- Cut 2 length-grain strips 3½″ × 42″; add to the top and bottom. The quilt now measures 42″ × 42″ unfinished.

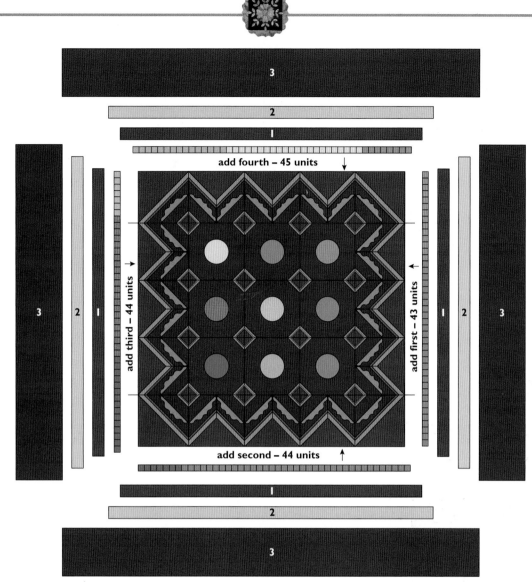

add fourth – 45 units

add third – 44 units

add first – 43 units

add second – 44 units

3

2

1

3

2

1

1

2

3

3

2

1

Border sequence

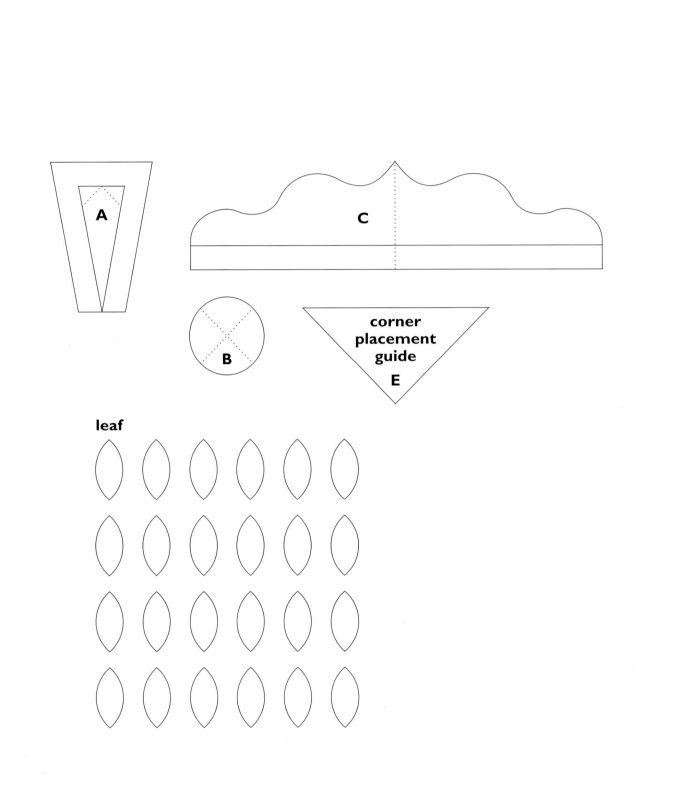

A

C

B

corner
placement
guide

E

leaf

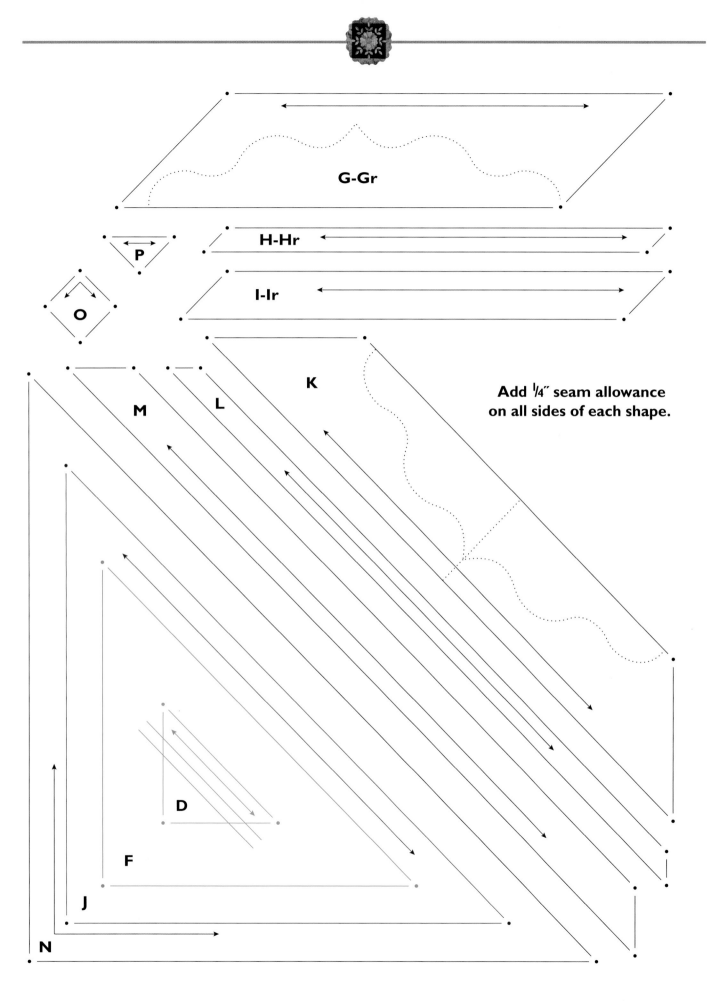

G-Gr

P

H-Hr

I-Ir

O

K

M

L

Add ¼″ seam allowance
on all sides of each shape.

D

F

J

N

Pieceful

46$\frac{1}{2}$″ × 46$\frac{1}{2}$″ unfinished

Designed, machine pieced, and machine quilted by author

Color

This quilt's color was inspired by a beautiful painting of Native American pottery and is described as achromatic, meaning no color. Blacks and whites and everything in between were used to create a very soothing, peaceful palette. For clarity, I will refer to light, medium, and dark fabrics when cutting. Use a wide variety of fabric prints (dots, stripes, paisleys, florals, checks, etc.) to create visual interest and enhance the design. This quilt would be just as beautiful in a monochromatic (one color) color palette.

Design

I initially planned to create a rectangular medallion-style quilt with a center design of three layers of stars surrounded by multiple pieced borders that would echo and enhance the center design by repeating fabrics, colors, and shapes. Because it is much easier to calculate pieced borders on a square rather than a rectangle, I squared the center rectangular design before adding borders.
Vital Statistics:
- Small Center Star Block Size: 3˝ finished, 3½˝ unfinished
- Drafting Category: Nine-patch, 6×6 grid
- Grid Dimension: 1˝
- Number of Shapes: 7
- Number of Pieces: 41

Techniques Used: templates (page 31), creating straight strip units (page 47), Y-seam construction (page 46), double half-square triangles (page 45), and rotary cutting (page 30)

Fabric Requirements

- 1½ yards total of light fabrics
- 1½ yards total of medium fabrics
- 2½ yards total of dark fabrics
- Final Border: 1⅔ yards of border print

Center Stars

Star 1

Make templates for shapes A, B★, C, D★, E, F, and G (page 108). Sew from edge to edge when assembling this block. Pinning at the dots will make positioning one shape onto the other for sewing more accurate.

★B and D are exactly the same shape; however, I created a template for each because B is a star point and D is background, so it creates less confusion.
- Shape A: Cut 8 from dark background fabric.
- Shape B–Br: Cut 4 each from light fabric.
- Shape C: Cut 4 from light fabric.
- Shape D–Dr: Cut 4 each from dark background fabric.
- Shape E: Cut 4 from medium fabric.
- Shape F: Cut 4 from light fabric and 4 from dark fabric.
- Shape G: Cut 1 from medium fabric.

Assembly

Piece the small center star together by making 3 different units. Units should measure 1½˝ × 1½˝ unfinished; the block should measure 3½˝ × 3½˝ unfinished.

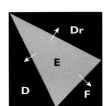 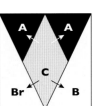 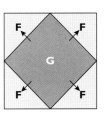

Unit 1; make 4.   Unit 2; make 4.   Unit 3; make 1.

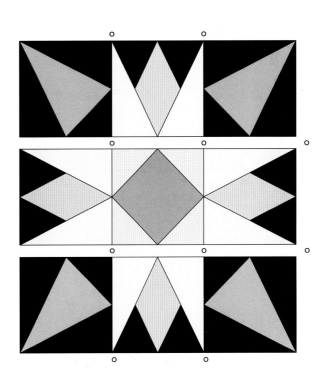

Stars 2 and 3

These 2 stars will be made simultaneously.

Make templates for shapes H, I★, J, K★, L, M1★, M2★, N, O, P, and Q (pages 108–109).

★I and K are the same shape, as are M1 and M2; however, I created a template for each as I and Ir are star points and K and Kr are background, and M1 and M2 have different grain lines.

- Shape H: Cut 8 from dark fabric.

- Shape I–Ir: Cut 4 each from light fabric.

- Shape J: Cut 4 from light fabric.

- Shape K–Kr: Cut 4 each from dark background fabric.

- Shape L: Cut 4 from medium fabric.

- Shape M1: Cut 8 from dark background fabric and 4 from light fabric.

- Shape M2: Cut 4 from dark fabric.

- Shape N: Cut 2 from medium fabric.

- Shape O–Or: Cut 2 each from dark background fabric.

- Shape P: Cut 2 from medium fabric.

- Shape Q–Qr: Cut 2 each from dark background fabric.

Assembly

Create 3 different units.

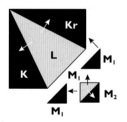

Unit 4; make 4.

Unit 5; make 2.

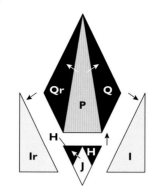

Unit 6; make 2.

Stars 1–2–3 Assembly

Make a template for shapes R and S (page 109).

- Shape R–Rr: Cut 2 each from light fabric.

- Shape S–Sr: Cut 2 each from light fabric.

1. Follow the piecing illustration and notice the 8 Y-seam areas indicated by a +, which identifies where to stop at the dot and backstitch.

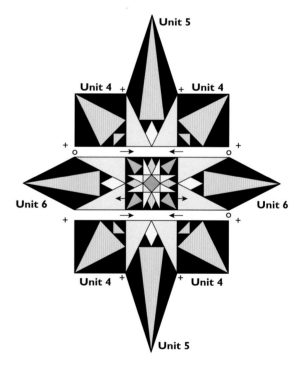

2. Fill in the star's edges by inserting shapes R–Rr and S–Sr using the Y-seam technique (page 46). The star measures 15½″ × 18½″ unfinished, from point to point.

+ = Y seams

First Inside-Corner Border

Make templates for shapes T, U, V, W, X, Y, Z, AA, and BB (pages 110–111).

- Shape T–Tr: Cut 2 each from medium fabric.
- Shape U–Ur: Cut 2 each from medium fabric.
- Shape V–Vr: Cut 2 each from dark fabric.
- Shape W–Wr: Cut 2 each from dark fabric.
- Shape X–Xr: Cut 2 each from light fabric.
- Shape Y–Yr: Cut 2 each from light fabric.
- Shape Z–Zr: Cut 8 each from strip unit.
- Shape AA–AAr: Cut 2 each from strip unit.
- Shape BB: Cut 2 from strip unit.
- Shape CC: Cut 4 squares 2″ × 2″ from dark fabric.

Strip Unit

Cut 6 strips 1⅛″ × 40″ from dark fabric.

Cut 3 strips ¾″ × 40″ from light fabric (this strip creates the light "inside corner" design border).

1. Join a dark strip on each side of the light strip to create a strip unit that measures 2″ wide from edge to edge. Refer to Creating Straight Strip Units (page 47). Make 3.

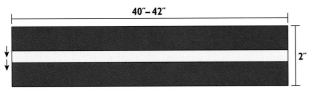

Strip unit; make 4.

2. Join T to V and Tr to Vr. Make 2 each.

3. Join X to Z and Xr to Zr. Make 2 each.

4. Join AA to Z and AAr to Zr. Make 2 each.

5. Join AA/Z to X/Z and AAr/Zr to Xr/Zr. Make 2 each.

6. Add AA/Z/X/Z to T/V and AAr/Zr/Xr/Zr to Tr/Vr. Make 2 each.

7. Join U to W and Ur to Wr. Make 2 each.

8. Join Y to Zr and Yr to Z. Make 2 each (you should have 2 Z and 2 Zr remaining).

9. Join Y/Zr to U/W and Yr/Z to Ur/Wr. Make 2 each.

10. Add each of the 8 units to the edge of the star individually, pinning and sewing from dot to dot. Refer to Y-Seam Construction (page 46). Once the units are all added to the edge, sew the 8 Y-seams from the outside edge inward to the dot and backstitch, matching all seam intersections. The quilt top measures 18½″ × 21½″ unfinished.

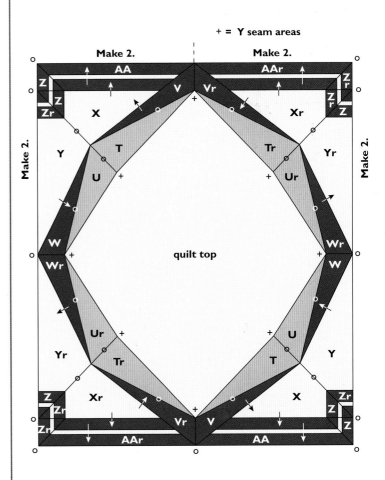

+ = Y seam areas

11. Add a Z and Zr to each end of the 2 BB strip units.

12. Add a CC 2″ square to each end of both Z/BB/Zr units.

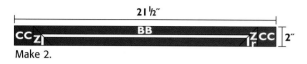

Make 2.

13. Add the 2 BB/Z/Zr/CC units to each side of the quilt top. The quilt is now 21½″ × 21½″ unfinished.

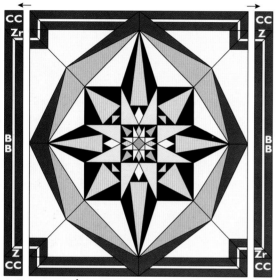

Quilt is now 21½″ square.

Borders

Spacer Border 1

I added a ½″ finished spacer border to float and define the star design and inside-corner border area.

- Cut 2 strips 1″ × 21½″ from dark fabric; add to the sides and press the seams open.

- Cut 2 strips 1″ × 22½″ from dark fabric; add to the top and bottom. The quilt measures 22½″ × 22½″ unfinished.

Chain-of-Squares Border

Make a template for shapes DD, EE, FF, GG, HH, II, JJ, and KK (page 111).

Noteworthy

Position all pins perpendicular to the quilt edge when adding pieced borders to the quilt; place the pieced border on top.

- Shape DD: Cut 64 from dark background fabric.

- Shape EE–EEr: Cut 8 each from dark background fabric.

- Shape FF: Cut 4 from medium fabric.

- Shape GG: Cut 40 from light fabric.

- Shape HH: Cut 36 from medium fabric.

- Shape II: Cut 64 from dark background fabric.

- Shape JJ: Cut 32 from dark background fabric.

- Shape KK: Cut 16 from dark background fabric.

1. Create this border from 3 units.

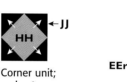

Corner unit; make 4.

Unit 2; make 4.

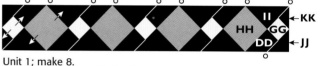

Unit 1; make 8.

Chain of squares

2. Sew a unit 1 onto each end of a unit 2. Make 4.

3. Sew a unit 1/unit 2/unit 1 onto each side of the quilt top.

4. Add a corner unit onto each end of the 2 remaining unit 1/unit 2/unit 1s. Make 2.

Spacer border and chain-of-squares border added

5. Sew a corner unit/unit 1/unit 2/unit 1/corner unit to the top and bottom of the quilt top (page 104). The quilt now measures 25½″ × 25½″ unfinished.

Spacer Border 2

This time the spacer border serves to bring the quilt to a size that accommodates the next pieced border as well as isolating this center design area from the succeeding 4 borders.

- Cut 2 strips 1″ × 25½″ from dark fabric for the sides.
- Cut 2 strips 1″ × 26½″ from dark fabric for the top and bottom.

Add the side borders and the top and bottom borders as you did for spacer border 1 (page 104). The quilt now measure 26½″ × 26½″ unfinished.

Flying Geese Border

This border is created using the double half-square triangle and sew-and-flip technique (page 45). You will need 96 Flying Geese units, 4 corner units, and 4 center units.

Flying Geese border

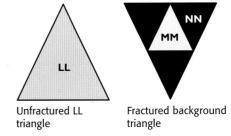

Make 96.

Make 8 (4 centers and 4 corners).

Noteworthy

The goose unit never changes its size from the rectangle you start with and the corner and center units remain the size of the larger square, EXACTLY.

1″ grid dimension

- Cut 96 rectangles 2½″ × 1½″ from light fabric.
- Cut 8 squares 2½″ × 2½″ from light fabric.
- Cut 224 squares 1½″ × 1½″ from dark fabric.

1. Make 96 Flying Geese units.

2. Make 8 corner/center units.

3. Join 8 sets of 12 geese each and press toward the point.

4. Add a 12-geese unit on 2 sides of a center unit. Make 4. Notice direction of geese.

5. Add a geese/center/geese border to 2 sides of the quilt.

6. Add a corner unit to each end of the 2 remaining geese/center/geese units and add to the top and bottom of the quilt. The quilt measures 30½″ × 30½ unfinished.

Spacer border 2 and Flying Geese border added

Tall Dogtooth Variation Border

The variation in this pieced border is that half the triangles (the background dark ones) have been fractured into 4 smaller triangles.

Unfractured LL triangle

Fractured background triangle

Make templates for LL, MM, NN, OO, PP, and QQ (page 111).

- Shape LL: Cut 60 from medium fabric.
- Shape MM: Cut 64 from strip unit.
- Shape NN: Cut 128 from dark fabric.
- Shape OO: Cut 8 from dark fabric.
- Shape PP: Cut 4 from medium fabric.
- Shape QQ: Cut 4 from dark fabric.

- Strip Unit: Cut 8 strips 1¾″ × 40″ (4 from dark fabric and 2 from 2 different light fabrics; I used 1 dark with 2 different light fabrics).

1. Sew 4 strip units of dark/light together.

2. Place the MM template on the strip unit, aligning the seam with the line on the template, and cut 32 from each fabric pairing for a total of 64.

Make 4 strips units. Cut 32 MMs from each fabric pairing.

3. Join an NN on each side of 64 MMs, using the LL template to monitor accuracy.

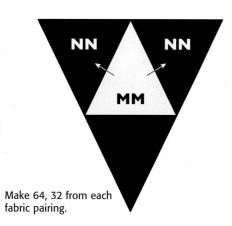

Make 64, 32 from each fabric pairing.

4. Beginning with MM/NN, join 16 MM/NNs alternating fabric pairings with 15 LLs. Make 4. Press toward LL.

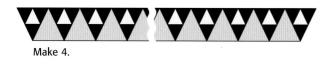

Make 4.

5. To make the 4 corner units, join 2 OOs to the 4 PP diamonds and add a QQ triangle. Make 4.

6. Add an OO/PP/QQ unit to the left end of all 4 border units. Press the seams open.

7. Add a border to all 4 edges of the quilt top, pinning at the ends and corner dots and adding additional pins as needed for smooth sewing. Complete the Y-seam. Press open. The quilt measures 34½″ × 34½″ unfinished.

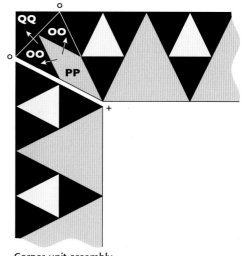

Corner unit assembly

Inside-Corner Border

This border echoes the initial inside-corner border, contains the series of pieced borders, and adds balance to the quilt design.

- Cut 4 strips 1⅝″ × 34½″ from dark fabric for sides.
- Cut 4 strips ⅞″ × 34½″ from light fabric for sides.
- Cut 4 squares 1⅝″ × 1⅝″ from dark fabric for corners.
- Cut 4 rectangles ⅞″ × 1⅝″ from light fabric for corners.
- Cut 4 rectangles ⅞″ × 2″ from light fabric for corners.

1. Join a dark and a light strip. Make 4.

Make 4.

2. Add 2 borders to the sides of the quilt, taking care to position them so that the wider dark strip is sewn to the quilt edge. Press toward the border.

3. Add a ⅞″ × 1⅝″ light rectangle to 1 edge of the 4 dark 1⅝″ × 1⅝″ corner squares. Press toward the light.

4. Add a ⅞″ × 2″ light rectangle to the adjoining edges of the 4 corner squares. Press toward the light.

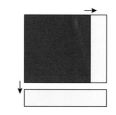 

Corner; make 4.

5. Add a corner square to each end of the top and bottom borders. Press away from the corner.

6. Add the top and bottom borders to the quilt top, which now measures 37½″ × 37½″ unfinished.

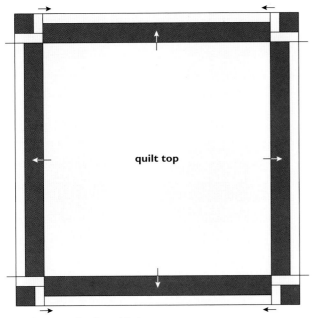

quilt top

Inside-corner border added

Final Mitered Symmetrical Border-Print Border

This border is 4½″ wide, finished. To interview 2 corner design options, refer to *French Confection,* Steps 1 and 2 (page 64).

1. Once you have chosen a corner design, cut 4 strips from your border print fabric 5″ × 56½″ (37½″ plus twice the width of the border (9″) plus 10″ for excess and mitering). Clearly identify the width of the design area you wish to see in your quilt, plus ¼″ at each edge for seam allowances.

2. On the wrong side of the quilt, mark the center of all 4 sides and make a dot ¼″ from both edges at each corner; this is the miter point.

3. Fold each border strip in half to identify its center. Then, on the wrong side, identify and mark (based on your interviewing process earlier) either the center of a motif or the area between 2 motifs closest to the center fold.

4. Measure out from that point one-half the finished width of the quilt (half of 37″ is 18½″) in both directions and make a mark ¼″ from the edge. It should be at the exact same place at both ends. This is the miter point.

5. Refer to *French Confection,* Adding the Borders, Steps 1 and 2 (page 65) to add the borders.

6. Refer to *French Confection,* Forming the Mitered Corners by Hand, Steps 1–4 (page 66) to miter the corners.

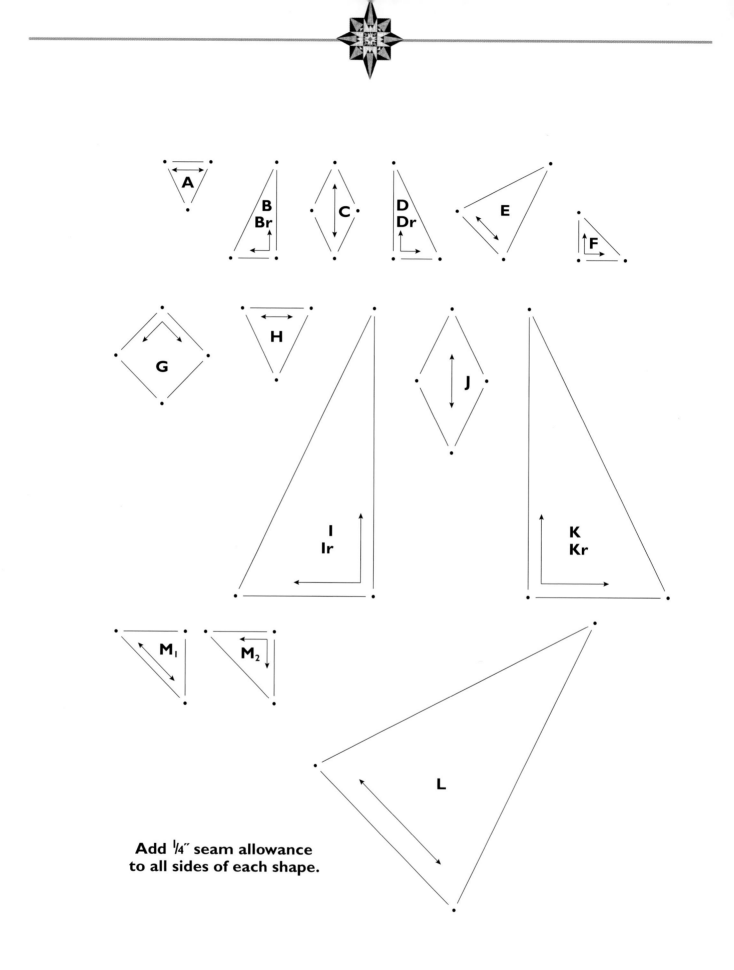

Add ¼″ seam allowance to all sides of each shape.

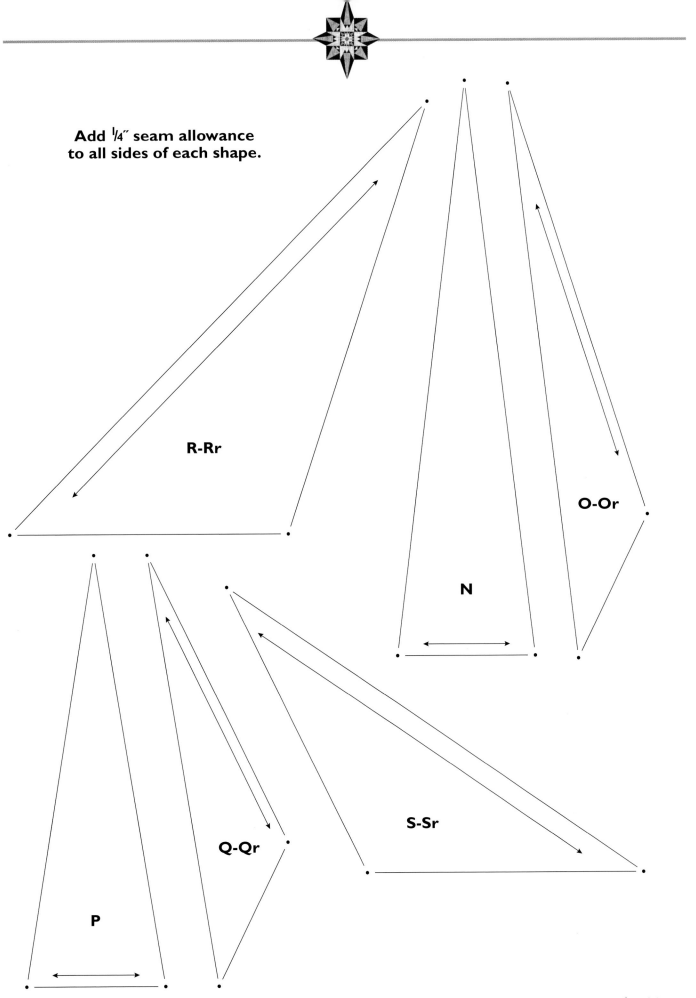

Add ¼″ seam allowance to all sides of each shape.

R-Rr

O-Or

N

S-Sr

Q-Qr

P

Add ¼″ seam allowance to all sides of each shape.

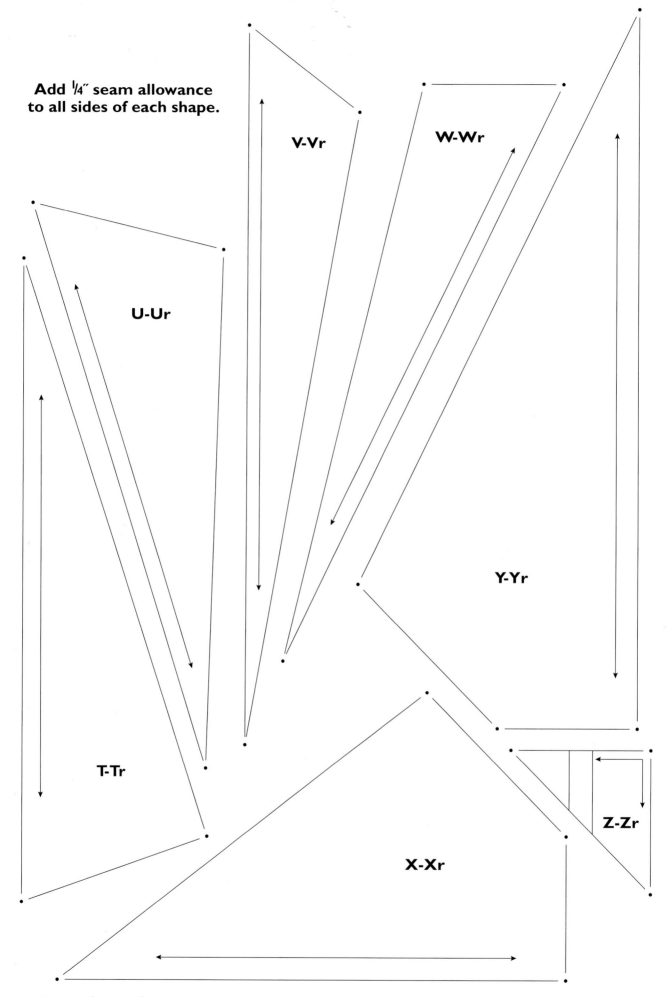

V-Vr

W-Wr

U-Ur

Y-Yr

T-Tr

Z-Zr

X-Xr

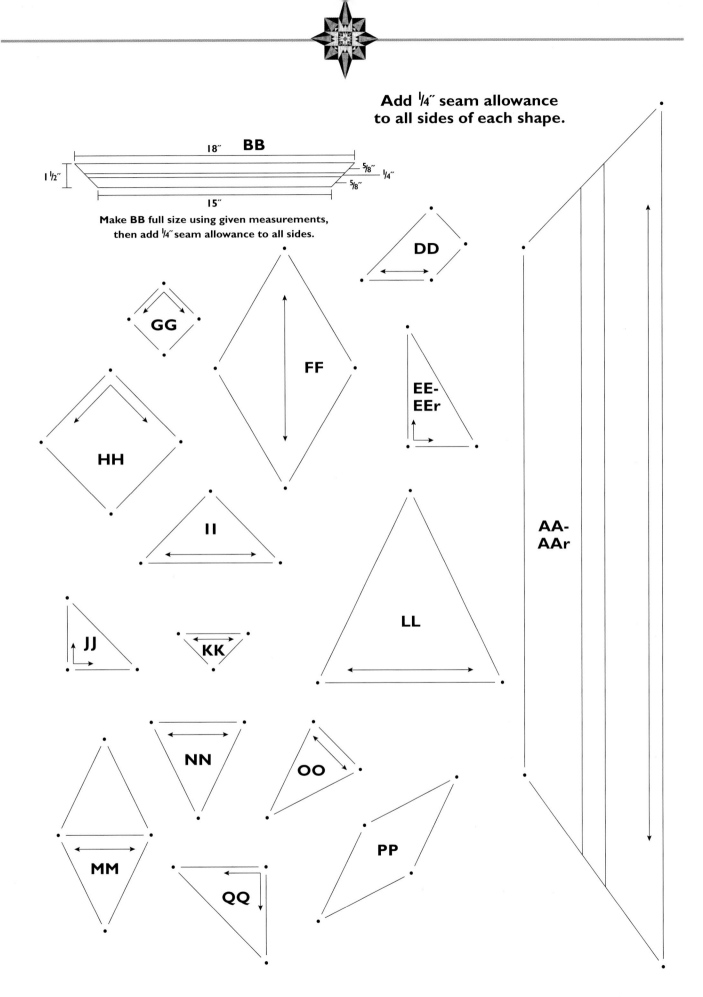

Add ¼″ seam allowance to all sides of each shape.

BB

18″

1½″

5⁄8″

¼″

5⁄8″

15″

5⁄8″

Make **BB** full size using given measurements, then add ¼″ seam allowance to all sides.

DD

GG

FF

EE-EEr

HH

II

AA-AAr

JJ

KK

LL

NN

OO

MM

PP

QQ

Lotus Flower

23³⁄₄″ × 23³⁄₄″ unfinished

Designed, machine pieced, and hand quilted by author

Color

To easily identify what fabrics and colors to cut, refer to the Fabric Requirements / Color Legend below. I used only six colors (I repeated the blue in the diamond). Sometimes I changed fabrics but the colors stayed the same. Use this idea but insert your own colors in the appropriate positions, so when you are reading through the pattern and it says, for example, "Cut color d," you will know what that is based on your legend.

Fabric Requirements / Color Legend:

a. Magenta, position 1: ½ yard

b. Green, position 2: ⅜ yard

c. Blue (used twice in star), positions 3 and 6: 2 yards

d. Yellow/orange, position 4: ¼ yard

e. Orange, position 5: ½ yard

f. Dark magenta, position 7: ⅜ yard

g. Background: ½ yard

Design

This quilt design showcases a Lone Star block to which a design border and a pieced border have been added. The center design is then placed on point and the corner-triangle borders are filled with design elements used previously. Two whole-fabric mitered borders complete the design. The repetition of colors, fabrics, sawtooth borders, and design borders, combined with effective value placement and contrast, allows the viewer to easily decipher the design.

Noteworthy

The Lone Star in this size (7¼" finished) is a challenging block. I cannot overemphasize the importance of accurate cutting and sewing; careful pressing with a hot, dry iron, as there is a lot of exposed bias; and monitoring and measuring your work.

A Lone Star block is derived from a simple LeMoyne Star that is created from 8 diamonds and then filled in with 4 squares and 4 triangles. The Lone Star design divides each of the 8 diamonds into multiple smaller diamonds—16 diamonds in this design. Unlike patchwork that is drafted on a grid of equal divisions across and down a square, the Lone Star is drafted from a circle that is divided into eight 45° divisions from the center

outward. Each diamond (45° division) is divided into 16 smaller diamonds that allow for various color/fabric placement scenarios. There are 7 color/fabric positions in the large diamond that can be interpreted in numerous ways, and you can use from 2 to 16 different color/fabric choices.

Design ideas

The 3 important circular positions are as follows:

Position 1 creates a small eight-pointed star in the center. The color and value choice here is important. A light value, especially if the background is light, could make it appear as if there is a hole in the center of the block. The 8 seams of the complete star design match in the center. Solid fabrics offer no forgiveness when sewing and require total accuracy. Prints, however, are busier and more forgiving.

Position 4 creates a continuous circle of color/fabric and is used twice as much as the other fabrics. If both the background color/fabric and this position's fabric are dark, it can look like cutwork. If both are light it can look like a halo, as is the case with *Lotus Flower*.

Position 7 creates the outer star points. High contrast between this color/fabric position and the background makes the star points sharp and complete. Lower contrast gives a softer, subtler look.

To interview your fabric/color choices and placement before you cut and sew, I suggest you create a rough-cut mock-up (page 26). To do this, make a copy or trace the diamond shape (template B; do not add a seam allowance) and use it as a mock-up reference. Start with a color idea or theme, perhaps a palette fabric. To make a simple rough-cut mock-up (no gluing right now), cut short strips of your chosen fabrics (⅜″ × 4″). Cut a 45° angle on one end of each strip and cut ⅜″ slices from the strips (because this is simply a mock-up, layer and cut several at a time for greater efficiency). This will give you the actual diamond shape and size for this star. Using the shape B diamond template as a reference for placement, arrange your small fabric diamonds on a possible background fabric. Remember that this is a mock-up; you will compose this star by placing and moving the fabric diamonds in different positions within the 1 large diamond and view it with mirrors by placing their edges on 2 edges of the fabric mock-up to see the whole Lone Star block on the background. Also, look at it from the opposite end (positions 1 and 7). When you are committed to your color/fabric placement, transfer your fabric diamonds onto the paper shape and glue them in place. Cut out the paper diamond, place it on other background options, and use the mirrors to be sure you have made the best background choice. This creates your color map for the Lone Star block.

Cutting diamonds from strips

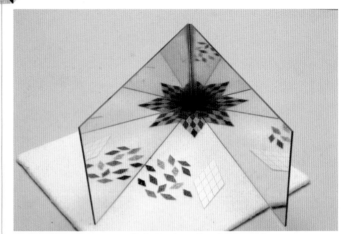

Placing diamonds on small design board and using mirrors

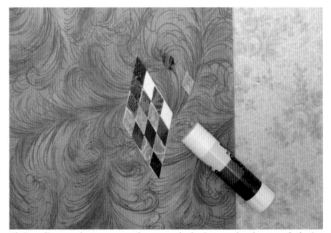

Gluing diamonds to paper shape and placing on background choices

Star Construction

Make templates for the A triangle and B diamond (page 123), transferring all lines exactly onto the B diamond template. Using your diamond mock-up for reference, you will create 4 strip sets or units from 4 fabrics each.

Noteworthy

The number of strips cut from each fabric is determine by how many times that fabric appears in the large diamond mock-up.

1. The grid dimension of the diamonds (finished width of the strips) to be able to measure your work (page 34) is ⅜″. Cut ⅞″ × 18″ length-grain strips of fabric from the following: 1 strip each from fabrics in positions 1 and 7, 2 strips each from fabrics in positions 2 and 6, 3 strips each from fabrics in positions 3 and 5, and 4 strips from fabric in position 4.

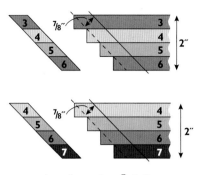

2. Using your paper diamond mock-up as a map, sew the appropriate strips together, offsetting them by the cut width of the strips. I recommend that you sew one 4-strip unit at a time. Sew 2 strips, measure, press the seam open, and trim. Repeat for the remaining 2 strips in that unit, then join the 2 pairs, measure, press the seam open, and trim. Two strips sewn together should measure 1¼″; 4 strips joined together should measure 2″. It is very important to the success of this project that you sew very straight and accurately, and measure as you sew. Press all diamond seams open and trim the seams. Refer to Creating Straight Strip Units (page 47).

Noteworthy

It is important to sew with an accurate ¼″ seam allowance, not a scant and not a personal seam allowance. When fabric strips are cut including a ½″ seam allowance, you must sew it off to create symmetrically shaped diamonds.

3. With the strip units right side up, cut a 45° angle on 1 end of each strip unit and cut eight ⅞″ slices from each, always keeping the 45° line of the ruler on a seam and the ⅞″ line of the ruler on the edge of the fabric. When both of these checkpoints cannot be arranged, the angle is off. Just reestablish the angle and continue cutting slices. Do not hurry this cutting process.

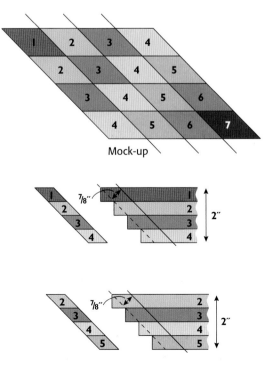

Mock-up

Strip units cut into ⅞″ slices

4. Referring to your diamond mock-up, lay out 1 large diamond from the 4 slices. Position 2 slices right sides together. To match each intersection, you must make a mark on the seam ¼″ from the edge on both slices. To do this accurately and consistently, use the B diamond template and align the edge of the template with the edge of the fabric and place the punched hole of the template over each seam. Insert a marking tool and make a mark you can see, right on the seam. Turn the pair of slices over and mark the same. Refer to Accurate Templates (page 31). Repeat for the remaining 2 slices.

5. To match the marks, insert an alignment pin (page 52) into the mark, through the seam, and into the mark on the second slice. The pin should travel through the seam, not through either fabric. Pull the pin so the head is on the fabric and the shaft is straight, not tilted. The alignment pin aligns and stacks the 2 marks on top of each other.

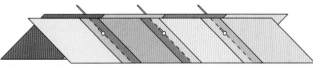

Alignment pin

6. To secure each intersection, place 2 additional pins close to each side of the alignment pin and remove the alignment pin. Place an additional pin at each end of the paired slices as well.

7. Sew across the paired slices and over the marks, taking care to sew straight and entering and exiting each edge at exactly ¼″. If the intersections are perfectly matched, press the seam open and trim. If any are not matched, correct them. See page 52. Two slices sewn together should measure 1¼″ from edge to edge.

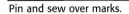

Pin and sew over marks.

8. Join the 2 halves to create the large diamond by marking, matching, and pinning the intersections as you did before. If the intersections are matched perfectly, press the seam open, measure (the whole diamond from edge to edge should measure 2″), and trim the seams.

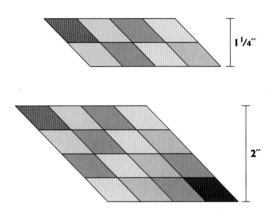

1¼″

2″

9. Lay the large diamond B template over the sewn diamond to check for accuracy. Make 8.

10. Cut 8 shape As from background fabric. Lay out the complete Lone Star.

11. Assemble the Lone Star, stopping and backstitching at Y-seam areas only, never at the outer edge of the block or the center edge of the block. Take care to match and pin all diamond intersections. Arrows ON the illustrations indicate sewing direction, arrows OFF the illustrations indicate pressing direction, plus signs on the illustrations indicate Y-seams, and circles OFF the illustrations indicate open seams. Always position your work to look just like the illustration. The completed block should measure 7¾″ unfinished from edge to edge and 7¼″ finished.

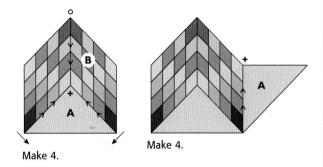

Make 4.

Make 4.

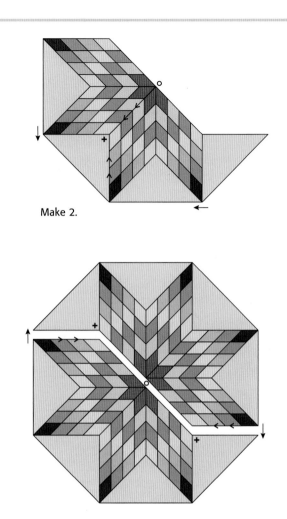

Make 2.

Assembly sequence and pressing path

Square the Octagon Shape

Make a template for the shape C triangle (page 123), transferring all lines and numbers exactly. Numbers indicate the sewing order, and lowercase letters indicate the fabric color.

- Color a (1): Cut 2 strips 1¾″ × 22″.
- Color d (2): Cut 2 strips 1″ × 22″. This is the eventual narrow (⅛″) border (page 53).
- Color c (3): Cut 2 strips 1¾″ × 22″.

1. Sew color a (1) to color d (2) and trim the seam to an exact ⅛″. Press toward color d (2).

2. Place color c (3) and color a (1)–color d (2) right sides together, with color c (3) on the bottom. Match edges, but sew next to the trimmed seam allowance edge. Press toward color c (3). Trim the excess to ¼″ from the last line of sewing. Repeat Steps 1 and 2 for the remaining strip unit.

3. Place template C face down on the wrong side of the strip unit, aligning the fabric seamlines of color d (2) with the lines on template C. Cut 16 shape Cs, 8 from each strip unit.

4. Pin and sew 8 pairs of shape C together and open the seams. Evaluate your accuracy by placing the shape A triangle template on top of the shape C pairs. Trim the seams. Refer to Both Seam Allowances Going in the Same Direction (page 49).

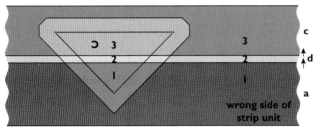

Cut 8 from each strip unit.

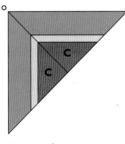

Sew 8 pairs.

5. Pin and sew 4 shape C pairs to 4 corners of the block that square the octagon. The block should now measure 7¾″ × 7¾″ unfinished, or 7¼″ × 7¼″ finished. Set the 4 remaining pairs of shape C aside.

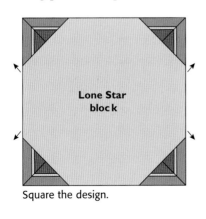

Square the design.

Borders

Design Border

Make templates for shapes D–Dr and E–Er (page 123). Transfer all lines on shape E–Er to the template exactly.

- Shape D–Dr: Cut one 2¼″ × 40″ strip from background color g, and cut 4 each of shape D and Dr. Pay close attention to the grain-line arrows and fabric grain when placing template D–Dr on the wrong side of the fabric strip.

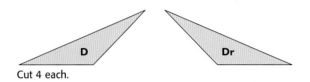

Cut 4 each.

Shape E Strip Unit:

- Color f (1): Cut 2 strips 1¾″ × 24″.
- Color e (2): Cut 2 strips 1″ × 24″.
- Color c (3): Cut 2 strips 1¾″ × 24″.

Noteworthy

You need a total of 48″ of strip length to cut 8 shape E and Er. This is slightly generous.

1. Sew color f (1) to color e (2), trim the seam to an exact ⅛″, and press toward color e (2). Sew color c (3) (on the bottom) to color f (1)–color e (2) (on top), matching edges but sewing next to the just-trimmed seam allowance edge. Press toward color c (3) and trim the excess to within ¼″ of the last line of sewing.

2. Place template E face down on the wrong side of the strip unit, aligning the lines on the template with the color e (2) seams exactly. Cut 4 E and 4 Er.

Cut 4 each.

3. Join shape D to E. Make 4. Join shape Dr to Er. Make 4. Press toward shapes D and Dr.

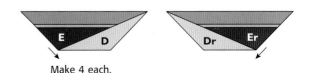

Make 4 each.

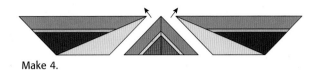

4. Join 1 shape D/E and 1 shape Dr/Er to each side of a shape C triangle. Press toward shapes D/E and Dr/Er. Trim the seams. Make 4.

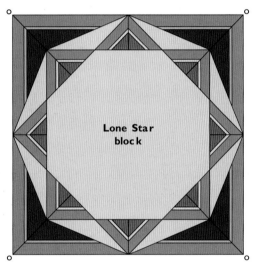

Make 4.

5. Sew a shape E/D/C/Dr/Er border to each side of the block, pinning at the dots, matching the points, and backstitching at each dot.

6. Sew miter seams by matching and pinning the dots and seams; sew from the outside corner to the miter dot, then backstitch. The block now measures 10¾″ × 10¾″ unfinished, or 10¼″ × 10¼″ finished.

Lone Star block

Adding the design border

Pieced Border

Sawtooth: Grid dimension ½″, 76 units total (18 per side plus 4 corner units)

These half-square triangle units will be made using the individual half-square triangle technique (page 40) and the oversizing and custom-cutting technique (page 40).

1. Cut 38 squares 1⅝″ × 1⅝″ each of colors a and b. Cut in half diagonally.

2. Pair and sew the appropriate triangles into squares. Press the seams open and trim the seams. Custom cut a square 1″ × 1″ from each. Make 76.

Custom cut a 1″ × 1″ square; make 76.

3. Join 9 sawtooth units in one diagonal direction and 9 sawtooth units in the opposite diagonal direction. Make 4 each, measuring as you sew, and press the seams open. When all 4 units are complete and measure correctly, trim the seams.

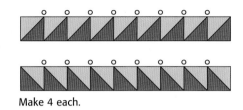

Make 4 each.

4. Make templates for shapes F and G (page 123).
- Cut 4 from shape F, color a.
- Cut 4 each from shape G and Gr, color b.

5. Join a G and Gr to each side of the 4 Fs. Press toward G and Gr.

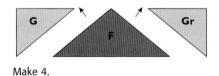

Make 4.

6. Join a 9-sawtooth unit on each side of the 4 G/F/Gr units. Take care to place them in the correct diagonal direction. Press the seams open.

Make 4.

7. Add a pieced border to 2 opposite sides of the quilt and press away from the sawtooth border.

8. Add a single sawtooth unit to each end of the 2 remaining pieced borders and press toward the corner units. Add to the top and bottom of the quilt. Press away from the sawtooth border. The quilt now measures 11¾″ × 11¾″ unfinished, or 11¼″ × 11¼″ finished.

Adding the pieced sawtooth border

Spacer Borders

Before placing the design on point, I added 2 spacer borders. One finishes to ⅛″ and the second finishes to ¼″. These 2 borders add detail and bring the design up to 12½″ × 12½″ unfinished, or 12″ × 12″ finished, which is a more desirable size for designing when the quilt is placed on point. Refer to Very Narrow (⅛″) Borders (page 53).

SPACER BORDER 1 (⅛″ FINISHED)

1. Cut 2 strips 1″ × 11¾″ of color e and add to the sides of the quilt. Trim the ¼″ seam allowance to an exact ⅛″ and press toward spacer border 1.

2. Cut 2 strips 1″ × 12¾″ of color e and add to the top and bottom of the quilt. Trim the ¼″ seam allowance to an exact ⅛″ and press toward spacer border 1.

SPACER BORDER 2 (¼″ FINISHED)

1. Cut 2 strips 1⅛″ × 12¾″ of color c. Add to the sides of the quilt, with spacer border 2 on the bottom and the quilt on top, right sides together, aligning the edges of the spacer borders but sewing next to the previously trimmed seam allowance edge. Press toward spacer border 2 and trim the excess to within ¼″ of the last line of sewing.

2. Cut 2 strips 1⅛″ × 12½″ of color c. Add to the top and bottom of the quilt, with spacer border 2 on the bottom and the quilt on top, aligning the edges of

the spacer borders but sewing next to the previously trimmed seam allowance. The quilt now measures 12½″ × 12½″ unfinished, or 12″ × 12″ finished.

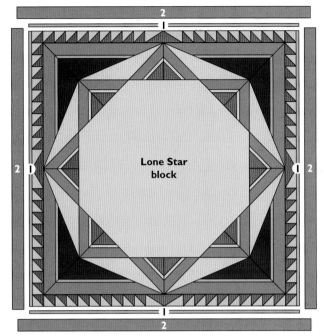

Adding border 3 (2 spacer borders)

Corner-Triangle Border

These borders will square the on-point design. With the exception of the sawtooth units, the design shapes within the corner triangles are similar to templates C, D, and E, although larger in size.

1. Make a template for shapes H, I, and J (page 123), transferring all lines and numbers exactly. Numbers indicate the sewing order, and lowercase letters indicate the fabric color. Shape H will be cut from a 3-strip unit as follows:

• Color a (1): Cut 1 strip 1¾″ × 42″.

• Color d (2): Cut 1 strip 1″ × 42″.

• Color c (3): Cut 1 strip 2¼″ × 42″.

2. Sew color a (1) to color d (2), trim the seam allowance to an exact ⅛″, and press toward color d (2).

3. Place color c (3) and color a (1)–color d (2) right sides together, with color c (3) on the bottom. Align edges but sew next to the previously trimmed seam allowance edge. Press toward color c (3). Trim the excess seam allowance to within ¼″ of the last line of sewing.

4. Place template H on the wrong side of the strip unit, aligning the lines on the template with the color d seamlines. Cut 8.

5. Pin and sew 4 pairs of shape H together, matching all seams. Press the seams open and set aside. Refer to How to Match Seams Going in the Same Direction (page 49).

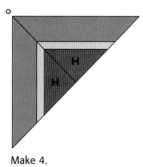

Make 4.

6. Sawtooth: Grid dimension ½″, 60 sawtooth units total, 8 single triangles total

For each corner triangle border you will need 15 half-square triangle units and 2 single triangles. Use the same techniques as in the pieced border.

- Cut 30 squares 1⅝″ × 1⅝″ each of colors a and b; cut in half diagonally.

7. Pair and sew 1 of each color 60 times, then press the seams open and trim. Custom cut a square 1″ × 1″ from each unit.

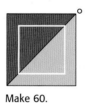

Make 60.

8. Cut 4 squares 1⅜″ × 1⅜″ from color a fabric in half diagonally (for the 8 single triangles).

9. Cut 2 strips 2¼″ × 42″ from color g. You need 60″ total, so you will have excess from the second strip. Cut 4 I and 4 Ir, paying close attention to the grain line of the fabric and the grain arrow on the template.

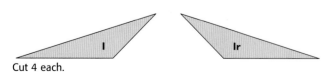

Cut 4 each.

10. Shapes J and Jr are cut from a strip unit. Numbers indicate the sewing order, and lowercase letters indicate the fabric color.

- Color f (1): Cut 2 strips 1¾″ × 42″.
- Color e (2): Cut 2 strips 1″ × 42″.
- Color c (3): Cut 2 strips 2¼″ × 42″.

11. Sew color f (1) to color e (2), trim the seam to an exact ⅛″, and press toward color e (2).

12. Sew color e (1)/color f (2) to color c (3), with color e (1)/color f (2) on top and the edges aligned but sewing next to the previously trimmed seam allowance. Press toward color c (3). Trim the excess to within ¼″ of the last line of sewing.

13. Repeat Steps 11 and 12 for the second strip unit.

14. Cut 4 J and 4 Jr shapes, aligning the lines on the template with the seamlines of the strip unit as with shapes E and Er.

Cut 4 each.

CORNER-TRIANGLE BORDER CONSTRUCTION

1. Join 7 sawtooth pieces and add a single triangle to 1 end. Make 4. Join 8 sawtooth pieces and add a single triangle to 1 end. Make 4. Watch the direction of the diagonals carefully. Press the seams open.

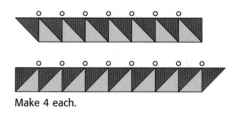

Make 4 each.

2. Add a 7-sawtooth unit to 1 side of a paired H unit and press toward H. Add an 8-sawtooth unit to the remaining side of the H unit and press toward H. Make 4.

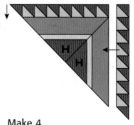

Make 4.

3. Sew a J to an I and a Jr to an Ir. Press toward I and Ir. Make 4.

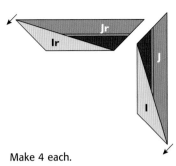

Make 4 each.

4. Sew one J/I and one Jr/Ir to the appropriate sides of a sawtooth/H/sawtooth unit; stop sewing at the ¼″ dot and backstitch. Sew the miter seam from the corner to the miter point, pinning and matching all seams, and then press the seam open. Repeat for each corner.

Quilt Assembly

1. Add a complete corner triangle border to opposite sides of the quilt, right sides together, pinning appropriately for smooth sewing. Press toward the corner triangles.

2. Add the remaining 2 corner triangle borders to the remaining 2 sides of the quilt. Press toward the corner triangles. The quilt measures 17½″ × 17½″ unfinished, or 17″ × 17″ finished.

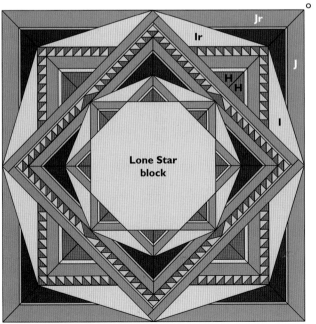

Adding corner triangle borders

Final Mitered Border

Two borders complete this quilt. One finishes to ⅜″ and the final border will eventually finish to 2¾″. They will be joined together and then added to the quilt and mitered at the corners.

- Cut 4 strips ⅞″ × 28″ from background color g.
- Cut 4 strips 3½″ × 28″ from color c.

1. Center a background color g strip onto a final border color c strip, right sides together, aligning edges, pressing, and pinning parallel to the edge. Sew and press toward color c. Repeat for the remaining 3 borders.

2. On the wrong side of each border strip, place a mark at the center. Measure out from the center in both directions one-half the finished width of the quilt (17″ divided by 2 = 8½″) and make a mark ¼″ from the edge.

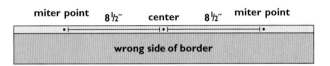

3. On the wrong side of the quilt top make a mark ¼″ from each edge on all 4 corners and at the center of all 4 sides.

4. Align 1 border with the quilt top, right sides together (quilt on top, border on the bottom), aligning the edges and matching and pinning at the center and ends and corner marks on both quilt and border.

5. Begin sewing just at the front edge of 1 dot; take 3 small stitches, backstitch 3, lengthen the stitch slightly, and continue sewing toward the opposite end. As you approach the dot, reduce your stitch length slightly, sew to the front edge of the opposite end dot, and backstitch 3 stitches. Repeat for the remaining 3 borders.

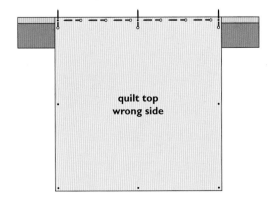

It is very important to align, press, and pin the quilt and border edges together. Positioning the pins parallel to the edge creates a flatter edge to sew. Remove each pin as you approach it.

6. Form each miter by hand (see *French Confection,* page 66), making sure to create a 90° corner. Once the corner is formed perfectly, press, pin, and baste it closed. Trim the excess to within ½″ of the fold. Repeat for the remaining 3 corners and evaluate carefully. Hand appliqué the miters closed, working from the corner to the inside miter point. Trim the ½″ seam allowances to ¼″ and press the seam allowances to one side; do not open. The quilt top is now complete and measures 23¾″ × 23¾″ unfinished.

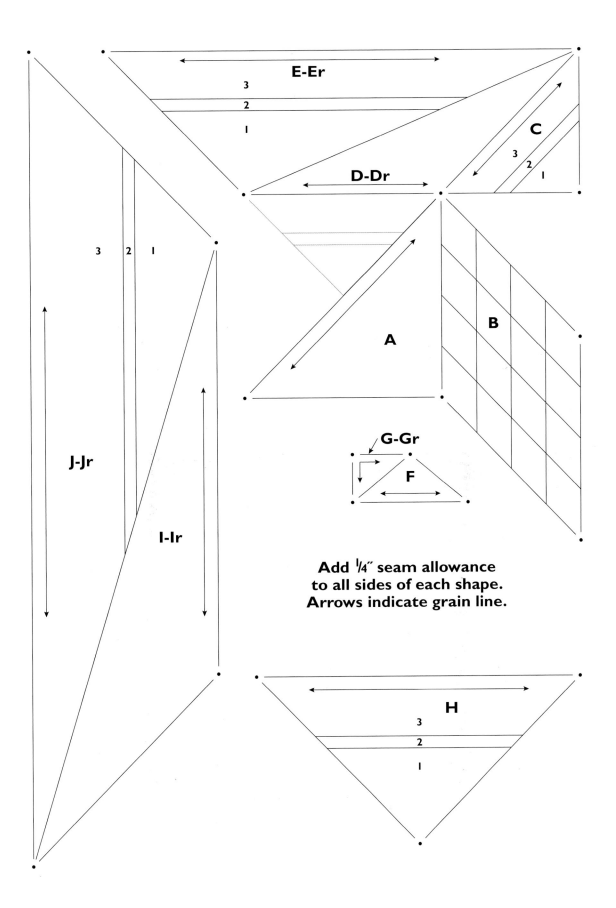

E-Er

3

2

1

C

3

2

1

D-Dr

B

3 | 2 | 1

A

J-Jr

I-Ir

G-Gr

F

Add ¼″ seam allowance
to all sides of each shape.
Arrows indicate grain line.

H

3

2

1

Sources

For more information, ask for a free catalog:
C&T Publishing
P.O. Box 1456
Lafayette, CA 94549
(800) 284-1114
email: ctinfo@ctpub.com
website: www.ctpub.com

For quilting supplies:
Cotton Patch Mail Order
3405 Hall Lane, Dept. CTB
Lafayette, CA 94549
(800) 835-4418
email: quiltusa@yahoo.com
website: www.quiltusa.com

For teaching information, a video, patterns, and supplies:
Pearl P. Pereira
768 Santa Barbara Drive
San Marcos, CA 92078
(760) 510-1832
email: pearl@p3designs.com
website: www.p3designs.com

For DMC Machine Embroidery Thread 50/2:
Ann Leatz
A to Z Designs (retail & wholesale)
402 Main Street
Dowagiac, MI 49047-1709
(269) 782-0635
email: A2ZDesign1@aol.com
website: www.AtoZdesigns.net

Bibliography

Barnes, Christine, *Color: The Quilters Guide*, That Patchwork Place, Washington, 1997

Collins, Sally, *The Art of Machine Piecing*, C&T Publishing, California, 2000

Collins, Sally, *Borders, Bindings, and Edges*, C&T Publishing, California, 2004

Johnson-Srebro, Nancy, *Rotary Magic*, Rodale Press, Pennsylvania, 1998

Jones, Owen, *The Grammar of Ornament*, Dover Publications, New York, 1987
(Originally published by Day and Son, London, 1856)

Squier-Craig, Sharyn, *Drafting Plus*, Chitra Publications, Pennsylvania, 1994

Wolfrom, Joen, *Color Play*, C&T Publishing, California, 2000

Index

About the Author

Sally Collins is an award-winning quiltmaker, teacher, and author of three previously published books, *Small Scale Quiltmaking, The Art of Machine Piecing,* and *Borders, Bindings, and Edges.* She took her first quilting class in 1978 and quickly discovered the pleasure and joy of making quilts. Although she is most recognized for her quality workmanship and teaching expertise, her continual interest is in the *process* of quiltmaking—the journey. She loves the challenge of combining design, color, and intricate piecing in a traditional style. Through this book, Sally hopes to guide and encourage quiltmakers to reach for their best and achieve quality workmanship.

Sally spends her time traveling across the country conducting workshops, giving presentations, and enjoying life with her husband, Joe; son, Sean; daughter-in-law, Evelyn; and grandchildren, Kaylin, Joey, and Lucas. Sally can be reached at www.sallycollins.org.

Also by Sally Collins:

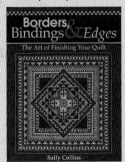

Great Titles
from

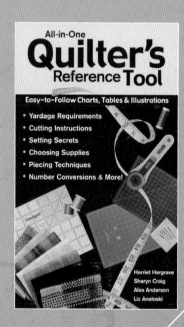